This book takes relationships to another level. Or should I say it gives you a suite hand on relationships. The casino terms work really well and provide a deeper insight as to how each of the players in education interact with one another. The Pit Boss and Player are not who you think they are. So, I bet you will read it and then give it to someone else to challenge them to go #ALLIN with you.

— RODNEY TURNER, MANAGER OF EDUCATIONAL SUCCESS, CLASSLINK

This book provides more than professional learning. It provides true perspective on what change looks like from the perspective of a classroom teacher and an administrator. Through open and honest reflection, readers are given a window into a system in flux and those individuals who were willing to take a risk despite their feelings of doubt. This book will help all empathize with the decisions made by others, all in the name of student success. It is more than a collections of thoughts, it is a powerful story of what can be done when leaders go ALL IN with the cards they were dealt.

— MIKE MOHAMMAD, SCIENCE TEACHER

All In has a unique voice that addresses many issues in education that deserve further discussion. By virtual fact that it is written in collaboration between a teacher and an assistant superintendent, it challenges us all to rethink and dream big when it comes to collaboration, creativity and change. The stories are filled with vulnerability, passion and honesty. The "ante ups" offer an incredible list of educators who continue to go 'all in' and who will inspire you with their stories. Thank you Jacie and Kristen for taking this gamble in sharing your stories with us and encouraging us to take risk, invest in ourselves and be brave enough to go 'All In'.

— LAURIE MCINTOSH, KINDERGARTEN TEACHER

ALL IN would make a great addition to your educational toolbox. I really appreciated the teacher and leader perspectives shared by Nan and Maslyk, as well as the practical and thoughtful ideas for how to collaborate, innovate, and do what's best for kids. Their storytelling style together with the addition of teacher and leader guest voices have hit the jackpot!

— JENNIFER CASA-TODD, TEACHER-LIBRARIAN AND
AUTHOR OF #*SOCIALLEADIA*

All In gives the perspective from each side of the aisle, both administration and teaching. We have the same goal to create meaningful learning for our students. This book shows how powerful positive relationships can be. We need to work together and be "All In" for our kids!

— RICARDO GARCIA, PRINCIPAL

This book portrays the development of a relationship between a teacher and administrator that offers a guideline for going *ALL IN*. It is amazing what can be accomplished when educators can be vulnerable and open to push-back all for the betterment of students.

— KELLEE OLIVER, COORDINATOR OF PUPIL PERSONNEL
SERVICES

ALL IN!

TAKING A GAMBLE IN EDUCATION

KRISTEN NAN

JACIE MASLYK

EduMatch Publishing

DEDICATION

To my <u>boys</u>... all three! My husband Eric... you are my rock. My amazing sons Trent and Jack... you are the reason I am the teacher I strive to be each day. The three of you are my heart, my strength, and my inspiration. Your unconditional love has been my guide while writing this book, and I thank you.

To my late mother in law, best friend and confidant, Sandy Nan. Thank you for always pushing me to go "ALL IN" with my passions for life. You believed in me. You never wavered. You gave me hope. The only thing you ever <u>asked</u> of me was to share my story with the world. Well, world, here it is!

~Kristen

I want to dedicate this book to all of the incredible educators who I have worked with over the years—the risk-takers and the disruptive thinkers who have pushed me to be better. I have grown so much as an educator and a leader because I have been inspired by you.
~Jacie

A special thank you to Sarah and Mandy at EduMatch for believing in us. You have created an amazing group of supportive educators and we love being a part of the EduMatch family.

CONTENTS

Foreword xi

Introduction xv

Bet 1: Mingle with the Players 1

Bet 2: Poker Face 9

Bet 3: Show Your Cards 19

Bet 4: Game of Chance 29

Bet 5: Feeling Lucky 43

Bet 6: Rolling the Dice 51

Bet 7: Pull the Lever 59

Bet 8: Cash in On Opportunity 67

Bet 9: Token of Appreciation 83

Bet 10: Million Dollar Decision 89

Bet 11: It's All About the View 97

Bet 12: What's Your Wager? 105

Bet 13: Go See a Show 111

Bet 14: Penny Jackpot 119

Bet 15: It's a Crap Shoot 127

Bet 16: The House Always Wins—The Ego in Education 133

Bet 17: I'll Raise You 143

Bet 18: The Eye in the Sky 151

Bet 19: What Happens in Vegas . . . 159

Bet 20: Double Down on Your PLN 167

Bet 21: Challenge the Pit Boss 177

Bet 22: Hit Me! 183

Bet 23: Join the Player's Club 189

Bet 24: Tip the Dealer 197

Bet 25: Beware of the Loan Shark 205

Bet 26: Don't Go Bankrupt 213

Bet 27: All In 223

Keeping It in Perspective 227

References 229
Other EduMatch Titles 231

FOREWORD

THOMAS C. MURRAY

Today's educators are some of the most talented, empathetic, hard-working people on the planet. Very few people in this world go to bed each night thinking about other people's children, but for educators, it's the norm. They give and they give and they give, often until they have nothing left. Educators will often spend more time in a given week pouring into the lives of others than they do their own families. They take pride in all they do and work tirelessly so that *other people* can be successful. Yet, ask an educator to take a sizeable risk, and as I can relate, many will freeze in their tracks.

It often seems that educators' brains are hardwired to be perfectionists. Whether it's the lesson plan, the professional learning session, or the conference presentation, they want things to go exactly as planned the very first time. I believe that this comes from educators having high expectations; of themselves and of others -- something that should never change. Yet, simultaneously, our brains are biologically hardwired to resort to safety. Challenging ourselves to step out of places of comfort and take a risk can be difficult, and quite often the fear of failure is a natural byproduct. As such, pushing our chips to the middle of the table and deciding to *go all in*, whether in our classrooms, in our schools, or in leading a district can be a very difficult choice to make. Fear can be so paralyzing, can't it? But as we all know, many of the greatest things in our classrooms, and ultimately in life, are found on the other side of fear.

We have to come to terms with the fact that as humans, we're going to mess things up. We're going to make a bad call. A lesson will fail. A presentation will flop. We'll say the wrong thing to a colleague. We'll take a gamble, and things won't go our way. It happens, and it's going to happen again, not just to us, but to those we work with and those we serve. Yet, failure is an opportunity for a new beginning, only with more profound knowledge and understanding than you had the previous time. Depending on your perspective, FEAR can mean Find Everything A Roadblock, or in the words of Zig Ziglar, FEAR can be the opportunity to Face Everything And Rise. Which lens will you choose?

Walt Disney, one of the greatest entertainers to ever walk this earth, was fired for not having original ideas and for *"lacking imagination."* Beethoven's teacher called him "hopeless" in having a future as a composer. The Beatles, rejected by Decca Recording Studios, were told they had *"no future in show business."* J.K. Rowling had a book idea about a boy wizard that 12 publishers turned down. These incredible individuals, who are now household names throughout the world could have given up. They could have allowed self-doubt to become the autonomous driver of their decision-making. They could have allowed the rejection by others to dictate their future contributions to the world. But they didn't. They continued to take chances, and ultimately, *went all in!*

Every day, teachers ask their learners to try something new. Every day, teachers ask their learners to take a risk and work diligently to push them out of their comfort zones. Ironically, many days teachers are fearful to do the same themselves. Fearful to try something new. Fearful to take a risk. Fearful to move out of a long-standing comfort zone. As educators, we can't allow our personal fears to dictate and limit the opportunities our learners both need and deserve. Our learners need us to *ante up!* They need us to take a risk -- a calculated gamble. They need us to be vulnerable. They need to see us fail forward. They need us to overcome our fears, and to watch us *push our* chips *all in -- for them!*

I have no doubt that, like me, you'll love this book. Uniquely written, and penned with humility and distinct purpose, Nan and Maslyk attack so many of the issues that plague educators today -- each from their leadership lens; Nan as a third-grade teacher and Maslyk as an assistant superintendent. Their relatable stories will leave you inspired and empowered with practical ideas, as they simultaneously will move you to challenge the status quo. They'll undoubtedly cause you to reflect on your own mindset and practices, and ultimately help you *go all in* for those that we serve. It's our only option.

The work is hard, but our kids are worth it. Now, go push those chips forward!

All for the kids we serve,

Thomas C. Murray

@thomascmurray | thomascmurray.com

Author of *Personal & Authentic: Designing Learning Experiences that Impact a Lifetime*

INTRODUCTION

True relationships are a force to be reckoned with... this very book goes on a journey between two educators destined to create change! As the **Pit Boss** in a casino is the overseer of the table games, **Dr. Jacie Maslyk**, Assistant Superintendent, provides a leadership perspective on the bets we make in education. **Kristen Nan, 3rd Grade Teacher** and "**casino player**," is ready to pull down the lever and take a chance at hitting the jackpot if it means making a difference for her students. Take a trip to "Vegas," where gambling and risk-taking are the names of the game. What bets will you make at the EDUCasino?

Relationships fuel learning — without them, we have nothing. A good relationship is more than something we want with others, it's something we need to be our best selves. It is a gateway to our happiness...the kind that is contagious. Valuable relationships are not something that happens in an instant, nor are they always easy to obtain. Like most anything that is of value to us, these too need our time and attention. They can happen in all settings and crossover throughout the chain of command. It takes risks and trust, but most of all, a mindset that is ALL IN! —Kristen

In education, we recognize the importance of relationships--with our students, our colleagues, parents, and the school community. Rarely do we acknowledge the importance of relationships with school and district leaders. This book is about the unique relationship between a forward-thinking teacher and a future-focused district administrator. By going "all in" with our relationship, we have begun to fuel change within our school district and extend learning beyond the school walls. —Jacie

Are you ready to bet on education? Are you **ALL IN**? This book challenges you to 27 Bets that should be made in education. At the end of each **Bet**, you will find a **Jackpot** filled with important takeaways to use starting today! Also, you will be challenged with a **Double Down** to take a chance that could create learning of epic proportions for your students, colleagues, community, and you! With a professional learning network built on change agents in education, we have also created an opportunity for you to see how other educators from around the country have raised the bar to **ANTE UP** for all kids! We hope that through our own risk-taking journey, you too can connect and hit the EDUjackpot.

Follow us on Twitter:
Kristen: @nankri120
Jacie: @DrJacieMaslyk

BET 1: MINGLE WITH THE PLAYERS

*I*t was a warm September day, and I was in the heart of my lesson when out of the corner of my eye, I saw someone standing in my doorway. I took a look, and to my surprise, *or possible detriment*, there stood my new assistant superintendent, Dr. Jacie Maslyk.

When an administrator is at my door, I shoot over to see what I did or what I need to do. And so, I did just that.

She looked at me and asked, "What do you envision for your classroom this year, Kristen?" I just stared. She had this grin. The kind that is like, well...**are you going to answer me or what?** So, I did... and I asked, "Are you being serious?" **UGH, did I say that to my new assistant super?** Someone I do not know. Who does that? I didn't even know her, but it is me. Me: Open Book. Real and Risk Taker. I'm me. Being me seems to be the biggest risk of all!

Little did she know, I had not been asked that question in years. Or when I was, nothing had come from it. This led to only one thing... I stopped asking questions. I stopped seeking permission. And even worse, I stopped taking chances. Opportunity was out of my reach. I'm not sure just when that truly happened, but it did, and it was crippling. How was I going to offer opportunity to my students when I didn't have it for myself?

> ❝**W**hen we stop taking chances, we simply stop learning❞
>
> #ALLinEDU

I remember laughing with my colleagues as we took in the advice of asking for forgiveness rather than permission. The laugh was half-hearted because we felt the true depth of not being trusted. If you had asked others if we were trustworthy, the answer/word spoken would have been yes, yet when we tried moving forward, we were continuously met with the word/action of no in a very untrusted way. I wish I could say that I was always able to take the higher road, but I am human and found myself breaking. I looked to bid to other positions or to possibly leave the district as a whole. I wanted to find innovation more easily. Why did it feel like there were roadblocks at every turn? Sadly, this didn't just end with me.

The power behind "no" stayed with me, and I found myself saying it more and more within my classroom and within my building. How did I take "no" and spread it like a virus so quickly? I had always been a YES GIRL! Yes, I can make that happen! Yes, I would love another student teacher! Yes, I can have that done in no time! Yes turned to NO. I told myself it was a compliance issue, *a form of respect* that I simply had to follow the rules, but was it? Was I being spiteful? Was I using my restrictions and limitations as an excuse for not being innovative? Did I take this word "no" so personally that I then stepped down from committees and took on the negative attitude of... get someone else to do it? What was happening to me? I don't suppose the onlookers saw this as clear as I do now. I love what I do too much to allow that to truly be seen. But I felt it. I felt it in my core. I am sure you could see it in my eyes. The glow wasn't there... the drive had been stolen from me with one repeated word... **NO!** The doors had been closed to my mind, and a lock had been placed on my heart. I simply wasn't ready to mingle just yet.

The Pit Boss Perspective

When was the last time you looked out at your casino floor and took an honest look at your players? Being the Pit Boss means that you have to have a sense of what is happening in your casino, at every table, every roll of the dice. The interconnected Pit Boss has an investment in every player, every game. It all starts with a conversation. A conversation builds into a relationship that allows the casino to thrive.

If your space is a classroom, a school, a district, or a community, take a look at all of the relationships around you. Do you take the time to check in with your players? What about the high rollers? Your high flyers, the ones who are always saying yes are just like the high rollers in a casino. Have you checked in on your longtime players? The teachers who have been a part of your organization for years and may require some support and attention? Do you make sure your teachers are getting "comped" like the regular players in the casino? If they are saying yes to every initiative and giving everything they have, then they might need some personal attention. How do you take care to ensure that ALL of your players are getting what they need? How do you welcome new players to the casino? How do you start a conversation with them? Find out what are they passionate about. Figure out what supports will help them to grow as learners and leaders. If you don't find out where your players are, then you don't know how to lead and support them.

How do we offer flexibility and freedom needed to be effective in the classroom? Do your players know that their ideas are welcome? Just as a pit boss talks at the tables with the players, do you take time to develop those conversations with others? Or are you standing behind the velvet rope distancing yourself from where the real action is happening

Don't be the boss suited up in the corner, never making eye contact with your players. Be intentional about creating opportunities for questions and conversations. Let down your guard and connect with the players who want to feel like their contributions are welcomed and necessary. What do all players need to take it to the next level? What can you do to help them go ALL IN?

JACKPOT!

Making time to connect as teachers and

admin is the first step in building a strong relationship. Having simple conversations can be the foundation for lasting connections.

DOUBLE DOWN

- What routines can you implement to ensure that you make time to mingle with all the players, regardless of your role?
- Take a step beyond and create an opportunity to connect with a player that you have not had time to work with recently.
- What conversation piece can you use to build a stronger connection with them?
- When was the last time you sat next to one another in professional development or for lunch? Can this be your next risky move to build a better relationship?

ANTE UP with Jay Billy

It is important to me that every student knows my name and who I am from the first day of school and that I know every student. I make it a point to get outside for morning bus arrival every day. Since our morning arrival takes about 30 minutes, I get to greet almost all of the students as they step off of the bus each morning with a high five, a smile, and a 'Good Morning!' Sometimes we handle important social-emotional issues that are happening, sometimes we joke around, and sometimes we play music and dance. Even the students who walk to school make sure they come and get a high five before entering. Once all students are in the building, I try to visit each class right away and check in. Unless someone schedules me for a meeting, this routine is another way that ensures that the students see me every day. I have to admit, this is my favorite time of the day and if these routines get interrupted, I never feel like I'm connected like I really want to be. At the end of the day, I station myself by the door and give each student (and a lot of the staff members) a high five as they leave. I make sure it is always paired with something positive like, 'Have a good night!' or, 'Get outside and play!' or 'See you tomorrow!' Both the beginning and end of day routines help me to be a visible leader. I can see who may be having a rough day (both students and staff) and who is ready for the day. I can have a quick, or not-so-quick, discussion with students who may just need some time before getting started. It should never be a surprise when the school leader is seen doing the things that everyone else is doing like bus duty, cleaning tables in the cafeteria, or working with students in the classrooms. We set the tone from the beginning of the day to the end of the day and we are responsible for making each and every day amazing for students, staff, and families.

- Jay Billy, Elementary Principal in Lawrenceville, New Jersey, author of *Lead with Culture: What Really Matters in Our Schools*
- Follow on Twitter @JayBilly2

ANTE UP with Martine Brown

During my first year as an instructional coach, I was looking for ways to engage the staff in my communications regarding emerging technologies and connecting with me as their partner in education. I was sending out emails; however, they lacked the flair and bubbly personality that I am known for. As I pondered, I decided to write a dad joke in the subject line of the email. The punch line was written in the body of the email and one would need to open the email to access the rest of the joke and the contents of the message. As I searched for short, school appropriate jokes that would be concise enough to garner interest while also helping me to connect with people on the campus, I was extremely nervous. What if they were annoyed by me? Will I lose out on making connections instead of growing relationships? Is the campus ready and accepting of out of the box communications as well as out of the box thinking? There was no way of knowing how the staff would react until I sent the message. The results from the one-liner subject lines were more than I could have ever asked for. I received replies with questions about the content. when I moved in the halls, staff members and administrators shared their own versions of the joke I shared or a new one. Instead of awkward ditties about the weather or educational backgrounds, these moments became a gateway for coaching conversations. The emails and more specifically, the subject line one-liner gave me an authentic platform from which to ask about curriculum and instructional successes or challenges. From this experience, I learned that taking risks in my practice must be purposeful, meaningful, and aligned with my professional identity and philosophy about learning.

- Martine Brown, Instructional Coach in Rowlett, Texas
- Follow on Twitter @mmbrown_brown

BET 2: POKER FACE

The Pit Boss Perspective

*P*oker players often sit around the table stoic, never letting the slightest expression reveal their excitement or dismay about the hand they are holding. Some prefer to not even talk to other players at the table, for fear of letting down their guard. The pit boss doesn't interfere, as these players take their game very seriously.

Mingling crosses over to all roles and all settings. It is a responsibility that we all need to share. As a new teacher, you were probably warned, "Don't smile until Christmas!" Once your students see you smile, you'll lose control of the classroom, and students will become unruly. They might, but not if you've taken the time to build solid relationships from Day One. We need to make sure that we are devoting our time to connecting with kids and setting clear expectations, in place of putting up our guard and creating an untouchable barrier around ourselves.

This not only happens in the classrooms with teachers and their students, but it also happens between administrators and their teaching staff.

Maintain a poker face.

Don't offer them inside information.

Don't cross boundaries.

Don't let them know the cards you're holding.

Why? This isn't a game. It's a responsibility to educate young people. This is not the time to put up walls and create barriers; it's time to break them down and make connections.

Sometimes the idea of the poker face extends beyond just your facial expressions. It influences your communication or lack thereof. It influences your leadership style. One principal in my past was the epitome of the poker face. She never smiled. She rarely talked to the students and only talked to the teachers if she had to. The majority of her day was spent in her office, behind her desk.

It may be challenging as an admin when maintaining a poker face has been the expectation. This may be all that your teachers know. This may be the only style of leadership that your administration knows, so much so that when someone new takes a seat at the poker table with a smile, walls are immediately put up. She must have an agenda. There must be some catch.

⚄

As a teacher that has been in the classroom for over 22 years, I haven't nor ever will understand the notion of "Don't smile until Christmas." I greet others the way that I want to be greeted. A friendly smile says everything. It is

hello,

I care,

today is a wonderful day, and

YOU make me smile

all rolled into one moment.

It is a way to express care and concern, along with a warm welcome into your very own world. Whether it is a child, a colleague, a parent, a staff member, or an administrator, I want them to feel welcome into my world.

Each day, you can find me at my door at 8:30. Yes, my principal expects this of me, but I, too, want to be right there to greet each child walking down the hall. I want to remind each child that I see them. I want them to know that they are important to me. Whether it is a greeting, a hug, or a high-five, every child that passes through our hallway is greeted by my colleagues and myself daily. The same rings true with the end of the day, as we are sending them on their way. All with a smile, loving each child becomes "bookends" to their day.

Beyond my classroom, I hope that my colleagues would say that I greet them with a warm heart each day... Whether it is a mindset of "Celebrate Monday" inspired my dear friend of my PLN Sean Gaillard, principal of Lexington Middle School in Winston-Salem, North Carolina and author of "The Pepper

Effect" or being a Joyful Leader like my friend Bethany Hill, principal of Central Cabot in Cabot, Arkansas, I try my best to inspire others to find the good within every child and within their day.

A smile can open up opportunities that you may have not otherwise have had. It can welcome others to be vulnerable. It can build confidence for others to approach you. It can let others know you are one word away from a conversation, and it can turn a not so good day into a bright one.

As I enter my building, I need the same thing as a child does, as every human needs... a smile. A smile goes a long way. It invites you into their world. It says, hello, without letting a single word pass their lips. It says, "I care" and "you are important," all in one moment.

Quite the opposite, a poker face leaves one wondering where they fit into the scope of the day or even one's space. There is a big difference in how I feel when an administrator notices me, greets me, and does it by name from the one that walks past me poker-faced as if something or someone else is more important. There is also a big difference in a "hello" that ventures out from a smile compared to one of obligation that comes with a poker face.

The effects of a poker face start at the top and are modeled for each of us to see and act on while creating an environment that is embraced. I've made a pretty big statement over the years...

I simply want administrators to do for teachers what teachers do for their students.

I want them to learn names, know something special about

each individual, relate, build a bond, trust, empower, acknowledge their presence... they (we) are important!

This particular statement has gone down in history as one of the boldest statements I shared within my district. This very statement led to a pivotal moment in my career where a stare down of poker faces left me in complete tears. It was not well received as it made its way to the top of the chain and ultimately led to what I perceived as a verbal reprimand (again, my perspective), but probably just a case of power, control mixed with humiliation that was "I will have the last word" kind of moment. My presence was requested to discuss my view on our culture or lack thereof. I was actually open to this face-to-face encounter. As uncomfortable as it may get, I felt it warranted our attention. I wanted to share my views. I wanted to be the voice for the many others that felt they couldn't approach our past administration to share something bold. To me, it was a game-changer. If my statement made others feel that uneasy, could that be because they needed growth in that area of their career? I was excited and ready to discuss change! I was not greeted with an open mindset at all. The poker face was on, and it appeared I was about to do a lot of listening. I wasn't really given a chance to speak that day, and after an embarrassing ear-beating, I left the meeting. I drove to the closest parking lot that I could find off of school property. I shoved my car into park, and I cried and cried. I had to let it out. I had to release this pain inside of me before going home to my sweet family. I refused to ever let my own children see this side of education. The glasses I chose for them were rose-colored... the kind that they could see all the good that learning had to offer. Not the disheartening side that had become my consistent reality all those years ago. The poker face I was greeted with limited me and in turn, my students. The door was slammed shut, and this pushed me back into my isolated corner even further. One that Jacie knew nothing about. One that I was not about to share, just yet.

Sometimes I wonder if the poker face was a technique that was taught in leadership preparation programs. There are some principals and central office administrators who have perfected this stoic look. Is the goal to create a barrier between themselves and others? Maybe the point is to convey an, "I'm the boss" attitude. Either way, it directly conflicts with the idea of building relationships as a way to move your school forward. Make a conscious effort to drop the poker face. Walk the halls of your building every morning and greet everyone by name. Offer a smile. Engage in encouraging conversations. What else can we do to dispel the poker face mentality? Have your morning coffee or breakfast in the cafeteria with students and staff. Being visible and accessible breaks down the poker face persona. Spend time outside at recess, playing kickball, or drawing with sidewalk chalk. Hanging out with the kids and being active during social times of the day shows that you care and want to have fun, too.

 **JACKPOT!**

Welcome all relationships by letting down your guard and look for the possibilities in every person and every day. Self-awareness is key. Whether your poker face is intentional or not, be mindful that your expressions are either opening doors or closing them to others.

DOUBLE DOWN

- Why do you think others portray a poker face? Why do you feel this advice has been passed down from teacher to teacher?
- How do you make yourself open and available to others to build and maintain relationships?
- How do you greet others each day? A hug? A high five?
- Do you have a special greeting that you could Tweet out and share with others to get them started? Be sure to tag us with #ALLinEDU

ANTE UP with Michelle Miller

In every administrator's arsenal of strategies is an array of practical ways to lead others. From open-door policies to visibility in classrooms, modeling a positive "can do" attitude, or celebrating successes of students and staff, a successful administrator needs a variety of ways to lead a successful building or district. A poker face, however, has no place in any successful administrator's tool belt, as it inhibits strong and healthy relationships that are paramount in effective schools.

As a superintendent, I find that relationships are the most critical to creating a positive culture and effective organization that is focused on student learning. To do this, I have found that an "open door" policy is critical. Students, parents, community members, staff and educators need to know that I am accessible to resolve or discuss what is important to them. Often, they just want to be heard and their feelings to be valued. A friend once called this the "Golden Robe" theory. I have found that his Golden Robe theory to be extremely important in my everyday work as it reminds me that I need to be welcoming and listening attentively to what-ever stakeholders need to say and a Poker Face won't make any person feel valued.

I also believe in a flattened organization where my administrative team is part of making high-level deci-sions, or at least, part of the discussion that helps the Board of School Directors or me in making important decisions. But more importantly, the capacity of a school organization relies on creating teacher leaders as well. To do this, we have to support educators in their professional development, celebrating their success and embracing their failures as learning opportunities. We need to recognize their personal and professional endeavors as well as those of their family too. After all, kindness matters and feeling valued by your co-workers feels good.

So as a school leader, my poker face is only useful when playing a game of BlackJack. I leave my poker face at home and just take a caring and genuine smile to the office and classrooms each day. It is much more effective and shows how much I love my profession.

• Michelle Miller, Superintendent in Hopewell Area School District, Pennsylvania
• Follow on Twitter @Vikings_Super

BET 3: SHOW YOUR CARDS

*S*howing your cards may look different at different levels and from different perspectives. For some, it may be as simple as opening up and allowing for judgment that could result in letdown, unsolicited feedback, harsh opinions, and even some form of reprimand.

Showing your cards is a form of vulnerability that is uneasy and at times, messy. Being vulnerable can be challenging at all levels and in a vast array of situations. For some, keeping their door open is one of the hardest things that they can do, and that comes down to fear of judgment. Relationships, or lack thereof, can make you feel like you just sat down at the Poker table. You wait. You anticipate. Your breathing feels a bit off. You look, and to your surprise...

Folded Hand

In my past experience, administrators usually stopped in with a purpose of observation, concern, or question, and all three of those reasons have caused discomfort. It has been rare, and often unlikely, that most administrators have had the time to come in just to see how I was doing or how my students were faring. I am not saying that there was not a good reason for this. I am simply stating that because of it, teachers such as myself at points in my career, have grown in fear and have closed themselves off from others. Vulnerability was not even a card to be played. My hand was not one of opportunities. I simply thought to myself, **I fold.**

The Hand I Was Dealt

As a teacher, I, too, have a variety of responsibilities that can be overwhelming and even debilitating. There are times throughout the school year where report cards and conferences can collide with a mile-long list of everyday obligations along with additional responsibilities that filter down throughout the year. These are not moments, but the hours and days of preparation when you want them to be most effective and worth it in the end. My students need me and my attention to come first, so I have to find a way to balance my own responsibilities with the needs of the relationships that I have created with them. I must be at the door to greet them and remind them that they come first, always. I need to notice when one of them does not make eye contact because their morning was off to a tough start, and then I need to find out why in order to shift their day towards learning. I must place myself alongside their learning and not remove myself to get my "to-do list" done. The bottom line is that when they are with me, they come first, and everything else needs to be second in my mind. Truth be told, I am looking to be part of my administration's balance and responsibility whereby I am a part of their world, nurturing another relationship that creates impact. I, too, need to be noticed when I enter the building or district-led professional development. I, too, need someone that is walking alongside me with my learning, allowing for vulnerability to be a part of the game. In many ways, our roles have more in common than not, and needs require attention at all levels.

Full House

To my surprise, there have also been times that the hand I was dealt with came with great excitement in place of fear. As if I pulled that last card from the back of my hand and realized it was the third card of the same rank that I needed. This rewarding feeling can ring true with the administration too. When one comes into the classroom "just because" and you sense that they are genuine and authentic. They are now showing that they are out of the office and in the same space as everyone else... the same playing field, one that is imperfect and built around trust. As administrators interact with teachers, they also build a relationship with the students and vice-versa just by being visible. Without hesitation, there is always a child that sparks a conversation or is looking for that little extra attention from an administrator. They are completely in tune with the novelty of their presence. I often stand in wonder, as I watch it unfold. It is amazing what children say when you take the time to listen. We want to be a part of those moments with them, not a sidebar conversation for them to see from afar. It is time to let us in, giving everyone a glimpse of the real you... the imperfect you that we can relate to! By being vulnerable and visible, we are modeling that we are one big family, that every member contributes and has takeaways regardless of our role. We must show our cards so that we can grow too!

Straight Flush

Jacie lays her cards on the table every time she walks in my door. There is no hidden agenda, no perfect execution of words, no mystery to solve, or worry that my students or myself need to shift gears. We simply smile and welcome her into our world... one she belongs in that has been built on vulnerability, risk-taking, support, and trust. Her hand is strong and powerful, yet open for all to see.

Five of A Kind

I am sure most administrators want this same reaction of teachers and students when they come to visit, but the truth is that it can only happen when a valued relationship has been built. It is the difference between a close relative coming to your home and one that has not had or possibly given the opportunity to bond with you. You are either running to greet them or stopping and asking yourself why they stopped by... is it a hidden agenda, or are their cards showing? To have the chance at the highest hand dealt at the table, you must take the risk and join in the game!

The Pit Boss Perspective

Being visible and present as an administrator is one of the most effective strategies that you can incorporate into your daily practice. Let's face it, you won't really know what is happening in your school or district unless you go see it for yourself. This might make teachers uncomfortable at first, especially if they aren't used to seeing administrators in their classrooms. Communicate that this is a practice that you will implement. Share with teachers that this is the way you will be able to observe the amazing learning happening within their space. Explain that this is one pathway that will help you to get to know the students. Our students. Ensure that this is not a plan to catch anyone doing something wrong.

Showing your cards from the admin perspective means being upfront about what you are doing and why. This transparency will show your students and teachers that your intentions are good. It may take some repetition over time for them to believe it, but it is well worth the time!

I stop by Kristen's classroom (and dozens of others) whenever I can. I have connected with her students and know most of them by name. That's important. The students have shared their Flipgrid videos with me. They've opened up in their personal blogs. I have read stories to them and planned lessons with their teacher as a way to get to know them better. It is particularly rewarding for me as an administrator to have the chance to work directly with students. When you move up the ranks in education, it often means that you become further removed from kids. I won't let that happen to me, so I try to get into the classrooms whenever I can. These informal visits allow me to reconnect with what it means to be in the classroom. It also gives me a chance to provide positive feedback to teachers about the innovative practices they are trying or the progress that their students are making.

Just as this is a chance for the teachers to show their cards, it's also a time for me to show mine. When I visit a classroom, I'm not a boss, I'm a member of the learning community. The students get to see me as an enthusiastic participant, not a stuffy decision-maker. They get to see how much I love maker education and the joy that I get from seeing them make discoveries in the classroom. I often take pictures and tweet out the awesome things our students are working on. I post student work and give shout-outs to the teachers that welcome me into their space. I'm not there to catch anyone doing anything wrong. I'm there to lift up the positive things that are happening and continue to build relationships with our students and teachers in our schools.

Jacie's perspective of "being a member of a learning community" has been the key to setting her apart from many administrators. She isn't afraid to learn alongside me, and for that matter, alongside students. Her own love and passion for learning are what ignites that very same feeling inside those around her. Somehow, she can find a balance between "managing, learning, and relationships," and because of that, she gifted others the confidence to share space in her world as an administrator. That space has now afforded me the benefits of learning, growing, and a relationship that is open to conflict, new perspective, and pushback towards a growth mindset.

JACKPOT!

Being vulnerable is one of the most effective ways to model risk-taking. It allows others an opportunity to recognize their own areas of strengths and weaknesses in place of compromising their own growth by allowing themselves and others to think that they have all of the answers.

DOUBLE DOWN

Learning is the most imperfect and priceless opportunity that each of us is given.

- What "card" can you show that would allow others (teachers, administrators, parents, and or community) to see a weakness?
- What about the strength that you possess?

ANTE UP with Tara Martin

Exceptionalities by Webster's definition are "characteristics that make us exceptional–unusual, not typical." We live in a world where exceptionalities are often viewed as imperfections or something to be "fixed" and require remediation. However, I've found that yes, my exceptionalities set me apart from others, but is being "set apart" a negative thing?

The cards I've been dealt cause me to think and perform differently, which is mostly perceived positively. However, I do have characteristics that are considered "flaws" because they require special accommodations to perform everyday tasks. For example, my sensory issues are burdensome requiring a heap of coping skills to do what others view as a "normal" daily routine. Yet, when I show my cards to those I serve, I am all in! They see all of me--the strength, the talents, the quirks, the overachiever, the curious creature, and the girl just keeping it real. I believe transparency is the foundation of lasting relationships. For when a leader is vulnerable and relatable, their followers feel safe to do the same.

By showing our vulnerability, our true cards, a culture of trust and belonging is formed, for without our unique combination, how might we win at this thing called life? Would there even be a game if we all had the same hand? I think not. When we play our exceptional hand, our God-given talents and quirks, we create a space where others feel valued for who they are and empowered to show their true cards, too. Be transparent. Be YOU. Your hand of life has set you apart from others, and that is not to be "fixed," but it is to be played. It's time to go all in!

- Tara Martin, educator, keynote, speaker, and author of *Be REAL*
- Follow on Twitter @TaraMartinEDU

BET 4: GAME OF CHANCE

*I*t started like a slot machine where you put your money in with just **a chance** at a return. Then it built. It spit out a small return, one that created a feeling of excitement. I found myself wanting to pull down on that lever one more time but was unsure if this time I would lose everything. I knew it was a risk. I had been burnt before. I knew that there was a chance that I would lose everything, but I just had to take it ... I reached up one more time. I put it all on the line. Life is a game of chance.... Relationships are part of the opportunity that moves you forward, closer to the jackpot!

On that day, an opportunity was knocking at my door. Jacie met me where I was at. My heart had been broken, and somehow, she knew it. I put myself out there over and over again. I felt the flame and had been burnt.

I am known to wear my heart on my sleeve... I gift others trust immediately until they take it away. I have always been that way... my cup is half full even when it is literally empty. My mind is wired for the positive. I have always believed that was God's gift to me. He created the tough path I would go down, yet He gifted me the best outlook possible so that I could see clearly along my journey. I am positive. I am trusting. My heart is yours. Maybe that is why it hurts even more when others let me down. When they don't give back what I am wired to give. Bottom line is, I trusted in the past to find out I shouldn't have. Was I able to do it again?

My heart wanted to ask, but my mind kept telling me, "Stop Kristen, you know what this feels like, and you don't want to go through this again... do you?" The easy way would be to keep doing what I was doing by living inside the parameters of a traditional mindset. Yet, my heart kept tugging towards a more innovative approach. A way to engage every child into learning while gifting them a new opportunity, a journey that would enhance every piece of literature and open minds to diversity by traveling across the globe and grabbing ahold of all aspects of learning along the way.

Hmmm... maybe I do want to go through this again!

Maybe it's my belief in the betterment or a need for excitement. Either way, I was intrigued that a simple twist on learning could light up an entire room. Even more, it can light up every child!

I have been known to steal 10 minutes here and there throughout the day to read a novel to my students when it didn't "fit the mold" of our set curriculum. My students can never get enough. Who knows, maybe it's because I strongly believe in becoming the character when reading to children. I mean, come on! Imagine the moment I bust out a book with a group of 8-year-olds that is set in The Great Depression. One that is about a kid living in the Ozark Mountains with *no technology*. A kid that wakes up and tends to the land before ever working on his studies. One that extends himself beyond all imagination to save his money for hunting dogs. One that had to save for two years before having what he needed to reach his goal. Based on experience alone, no one in my classroom could relate. No one comes predisposition to loving *this novel*. Yet, in the end, they do. Oh, do they ever! Love is the only word that can possibly come close to describing it. Oh yes, I'm talking about <u>Where the Red Fern Grows</u>, written by the one and only Wilson Rawls. The man that couldn't spell and literally burnt the first copy of his manuscript because he was convinced it was worthless.

This is a must, I thought! Sounds like a no brainer, right? Not! This was in addition to the obligatory curriculum built by the masses. The one that required me to be on the same story, on the same page, and assessed on the same day no matter what my students' abilities or interests were. This exciting adventure had been extra "work" as it didn't come from the "curriculum" that was being taught throughout my grade level. I mean, come on, it is a fifth-grade reading level for Pete's sake, and I **only** teach third **grade**! How was this going to fly when it has never been able to before. I could list 20 ways to connect it to what I was already teaching, but that had never gotten me anywhere before... why was this going to be any different?

I had to take a chance. No regrets. I was leaving it all on the table.

I went for it. I believed Jacie meant every word she said. She was right there beside me. Not in front of me, but beside me... where I was at. So, I did it... I looked at her and asked if I could step away from the anthology to conduct a 6-week novel study. This is something that I had asked numerous times throughout my career, hoping that the answer would be yes.

Trust is such a game-changer. It drives most every moment you create. You either trust yourself or the risk that you are about to take. You trust that there is something to hold on to... **or maybe someone!** Taking the risk is what led to the amazing world I had stepped into... one that I would take over and over again!

TAKE THE RISK

NOTHING AMAZING COMES WITHOUT A LITTLE RISK

#ALLinEDU

The Pit Boss Perspective

Administrators are not your friends.

You can't trust them.

They will act like they are supporting you, but when push comes to shove, they really won't.

Sadly, I have heard these warnings shared in several school districts. It is a destructive mindset that often prevents a relationship from being established between teachers and administrators. Before an administrator even reaches out to a teacher, there is already this uneasy feeling about motive, lack of genuineness, or mistrust. This can be a lot to overcome, especially with teachers who may have been burned in the past.

As an admin, we need to take a chance and move forward, building relationships every opportunity we get. We need to actively look for ways to connect with teachers. There is no doubt, we will be met with hesitation or even resistance at times. How might you bring teachers into the decision-making process?

Can you hold a "lunch and learn" session to bring educators together to share a meal and learn about a new tech tool? Can you invite a teacher as your guest to a leadership meeting that you are attending? Maybe you can co-present at a conference with a teacher? Blurring the lines between your formal roles can open up conversations and build rapport.

Find the informal ways you can get to know the educators in your district as people first. They are more than classroom teachers. Get to know them, and as you do, share more about the person that you are. The more you put yourself out there, the more you will strengthen *relationships with those individual teachers, but you will also build credibility with the other teachers who are looking within your district.*

*Part of being **All-In** means that, despite the roadblocks that may be put in our way, we continue to value the power of relationships with our teachers and work every day to build trust and understanding with the individuals who have the greatest impact on our students.*

Teachers play a huge role in forming and nurturing relationships with their administrators. They are either open to building bridges, or they are creating walls. Relationships cannot be formed with a one-sided mindset. The word "side" is used so candidly, and I am not above being one to have used it. I have felt the pains of being isolated as a classroom teacher, wondering to myself how "they" have forgotten so quickly as to what it is like to work with children one-to-one each day. I have placed myself on the other side of the room opposite of my admin, mainly because I felt it wasn't my place to be among them. Was it their business attire versus my casual kid-friendly outfit, or was it the lack of common ground in conversation? I really don't know that answer, but I am leaning towards my own ignorance in what I perceived to be a line that I shouldn't cross.

Why is there even a line to begin with? I thought we were all on the same team--putting kids first. If there are sides, I do what I can to blur the lines between them. Connecting with teachers and building

those relationships shows that we are working towards the same goal. It's not about the clothes. I despise wearing suits. I want to be approachable, not untouchable. It shouldn't be about the hierarchy. Yes, I have a title, but it's not that important to me. My role is to be a connector, an idea-pusher, a celebrator. I don't want to be a pit boss managing the interactions of the casino. I choose to be a player, sitting down and working with those who want to come and throw down a bet at the table.

Have you found yourself on **a side** in education?

Have you ever wondered why the other side couldn't appreciate your perspective? Why is that?

Have you ever created walls in place of building bridges?

If we truly want to give our children a better chance in education, we must rethink our own role and the accountability we must hold ourselves to. The only side we should ever be referencing within education is the one that we stand together on for all kids!

JACKPOT!

Take a chance and build trust with others, even those outside of the traditional boundaries of your role. The payoff will be worth it!

DOUBLE DOWN

- How will you go "All In" and take the first step towards building trust with others?
- How will you respond the next time you hear the words related to "the other side"?
- How will you build bridges in place of walls?

> **"T**rust removes roadblocks to powerful relationships"
>
> #ALLinEDU

ANTE UP with Michael Abramczyk

As a kid, school was not my favorite place. I was "that kid." I'm sure that you can see me, sitting in the back of your class, making noises, talking while you're teaching, falling out of my seat, losing papers, testing your patience. Every. Single. Day. "Michaels" were notoriously bad kids and the ones you had to keep an eye on *or at least that's what I heard throughout the first eight years of school.* I started believing that I was a bad, troublesome kid, and was looking for any way to fit in and be accepted. By middle school, I had begun to fully live up to my name, Michael, as the wheels completely fell off the wagon. In addition to these unsavory characteristics, I was bullied incessantly. To cope, I began to drink "while underage." My life spiraled out of control until I reached college where I finally got myself connected to a supportive community and began to rebound.

About 10 years into my teaching career, I received an urgent phone call from our curriculum coordinator, asking to speak with me. I was a little alarmed, but I proceeded. After pleasantries, she made her pitch, "Mike, we want you to move to the middle school." I was floored and quickly responded, "No. I cannot. I won't. I just cannot." I believed that I wasn't middle school material, and was terrified of reliving the turbulent years of my youth. I promised to think about it, but I wasn't completely sold. Later that night, I spoke with my wife and she encouraged me not to allow my past to dictate my future.

That fall, I pushed back against fear, stepping into the unknown, to boldly develop relationships with my students, fellow teachers, and the community. Very quickly, I realized that many of the students were just like me -- they had a voice, desired to be heard, and most importantly, they wanted to be loved and appreciated for what made them unique. As my level of comfort grew, so did my responsibilities.

At the end of my second year at Simmons Middle School, my administrative team approached me with an opportunity to lead our Drama program. Once again, I protested. I knew nothing about the Arts, except I didn't like them. "Drama is boring. I'm a sports guy," I protested. It was at that moment, my wife's voice redirected me: "Don't let your past dictate your future." In the Fall of 2013, I agreed to co-direct my first play with my colleague, Megan Hacholski. To say that we didn't know what we were doing was a tremendous understatement. Megan and I were clueless, but we did understand one thing: Middle schoolers were looking for acceptance, understanding, and a place to belong. With that mindset in our sights, we set "Family" as our cornerstone principle. We moved from operating as a simple after-school club with 40 kids to a powerful organization of 140 of the best actors and technicians in the southwest suburban Chicagoland area. To date, "The Family" is responsible for several Illinois State High School championship titles, many All-State performers, and countless young people who operate with EXCELLENCE as their standard as they strive to leave a legacy worth living.

As I write this vignette, once again, I stand at the precipice of the unknown, declaring that I am "All-In." At the height of our success, our leadership team has decided to walk away from our roles in our Drama program, each to pursue new adventures. While I do not know what awaits us in this next season, I do know that

I will not allow my fears of the past dictate my future endeavors.

• Michael Abramczyk, Creative Learning Systems STEM Lab Facilitator in Oak Lawn, Illinois
• Follow on Twitter @_on11

ANTE UP with Jessie Smith

Growing up and going through the educational system I had a specific point of view as the student. I sat at a desk that was perfectly aligned in a row, while the teacher stood in front of the room. However, as the system has changed over time, and I learned the ins and outs of the job, I never forgot those early years and my reservations about the system, or my grandiose ideas for changing it. I knew that this culture needed to be changed if I was ever going to get the results that I had dreamed of from my students. I was not sure how to start this process, how to give accountability and ownership to my students of their learning.

So in this situation, I knew it was going to be a gamble, but like I had done before I knew who to bet on: my students. I posed the question to them as they were the true stakeholders in the room. Once again, to my surprise, my students had a solution, they wanted an opportunity to teach the class. That's right; my students wanted an opportunity to be the teacher.

At first, I thought, "Oh yeah, okay." Then I thought some more, and I realized the times I had done my best learning were times I taught something to someone else. I looked at my students and realized this was my moment; this was my chance to show that I was not all talk in my classroom. I had to make a grandstand and relinquish my power and give them the reigns to try, to fail, and to try again. I left school that day racking my brain. I knew that I had to come up with a system, a rubric, and some guidelines and really think about how to make this a measurable and useful activity for my students. Once I had the details situated and a fair schedule that gave any willing student an opportunity to take a turn to teach, a way to measure the "student observers," I knew I was ready to roll this out.

I'll never forget the first student who volunteered; I am not sure who was more nervous...him or me! He collected the prep materials I had made, as was his homework assignment and came the next day ready to take on the role of the teacher. I had never in my life seen a class so engaged. I was there to help catch if anyone fell but much to my delight, my instincts were right and the class loved it. All students were supporting their 'new teacher', asking questions, participating, and more. I was merely a facilitator, sitting back and just guiding the class with the slight of the hand. It was one of the best classes I had all year and I couldn't wait to give the rest of the students a shot to shine. Surprisingly, during this lesson never once did I feel powerless. In fact, I felt proud and more accomplished than on a day where I led the class. I learned in that quick hour, that teaching was never about being the leader in the front. It was about showing my students that they had the power all within themselves. Once I made the day less about me, I found the results that I had always been hoping for. I realized how many other techniques and ideas did my students had that I had not given ear to before. Well, now that I know that, there was no going back. In room 1614 we have upped the ante, and want to know who's in.

• Jessie Smith, Middle School Teacher in Rochester, Pennsylvania
• Follow on Twitter @Miss_SmithRASD

BET 5: FEELING LUCKY

$\mathcal{A}$ll I wanted to do was take my students on an adventure with an incredible piece of literature. I decided I had to ask. There was that look again, that grin or maybe look of, what are you thinking? The one that made me a bit uneasy. It was the grin of... I just asked something rather stupid. She said, "Why not?" Yes, that is what she said...WHY NOT? For real? Is this a trick? Are you setting me up so that I am called out on my ideas again to explain why I feel it is so important to give children opportunities to take risks, to learn from others beyond me? Did she really just say that?

Yes, all these thoughts rolled through my mind. Sorry, not sorry that I am calling it out. That I have tried to fight for my students' voice over and over to be told that I had a job to do... (my interpretation) to be compliant, earn my pay, and prepare our children for the assessment that would ultimately reflect their ability and the district's reputation. Will I stay in this mindset? Will I continue to fear the disappointment others have had towards me? Will I allow their strong views to dictate what I feel is best for kids? No! I simply can't! She was willing to meet me where I was at, and now, I was ready to gift it to my students. I was feeling lucky!

This was an opportunity for them to see that the love of reading can be an adventure. This was my chance to create an experience beyond the status quo that I had been executing through professional compliance for way too long. This was an opportunity to embrace all components of a book and bring each one to life so that each child could feel the true depths of literature. This was a way for me to bring meaning to the skills that my students needed to master.

In place of cramming this magnificent novel in between the scheduling of isolated stories, each day would become the setting, we would feel the mood of each chapter, and embrace the internal conflict of each character as it unfolded. We would predict the problems that would be faced and create solutions to compare and contrast with those that unraveled. We would be embracing the love of reading in the most authentic way possible.

I didn't hesitate. I built a complete novel study that was tied to the standards to which I was responsible for teaching. I shared them with my students and their parents. I was on fire! I was free! I was trusted. I was teaching again! I was all in!

The Pit Boss Perspective

Why is compliance valued in education? This traditional look at teaching and learning requires that students consume and comply, as opposed to think, push, and innovate. This system of compliance over creation has put us in a sad state of affairs. It has stifled our students and drained our teachers, but yet it keeps on happening in schools and districts everywhere.

This was the exact situation we were in. There was a passionate teacher in front of me aching to do the work that she loved, that she was good at, that would awaken the minds and hearts of her students. What was I going to say? No? "Please keep trudging through the manual, oh compliant soldier. Continue to prepare students for the standardized test that doesn't measure how creative, empathetic, and curious your students are." Heck, no!

I am looking for the disrupters, the teachers who look at the current status of education and say--No! We are not going to continue on in this way. We are committed to doing better for kids. Sometimes these teachers are out on their own, pushing the limits. They make it happen for their students, no matter what it takes. Often, they are doing it behind closed doors with no support at all. I had to get out there and find out what I could do to help our teachers to take the next step.

And Kristen, she was ready to take those steps with me. Our relationship started that day in her classroom when we realized that we both wanted great things for kids and that we weren't going to let tradition, compliance, or complacency get in our way!

Other teachers were ready too. Some wanted the chance to incorporate more creative projects into their physics class. Others wanted to try co-teaching with their colleagues. Some just wanted the chance to change around their classroom space and make it more responsive to the needs of their students. As I continued to have conversations with teachers, I have tried to meet them where they're at and give them an encouraging nudge to do whatever they are longing to do.

As a new district administrator, I promised myself that I would make relationships a priority. Every step up the ladder in education often takes you further away from kids and teachers. As a former elementary principal, the connections that I had with parents, students, and teachers were paramount to my success. As an assistant superintendent, how would I maintain that? Over the summer, I studied our school yearbooks to learn the names and roles of the teachers. I was committed to learning who everyone was before they started the school year.

In my first few weeks, I visited all of the buildings and talked with students and teachers.

The role of the pit boss is to oversee operations on the casino floor, spending much of the time circulating among the tables and monitoring customers to ensure everyone "plays by the rules."

This is similar to a district administrator--get out to the buildings (the casino floor) circulate among the tables (classrooms) and oversee the players (teachers, staff, and students). While I am viewed as one who monitors, my goal is not simply to circulate and monitor but to connect, communicate, and motivate.

However, I wasn't looking for people playing by the rules like a pit boss. It was quite the opposite. I was looking for the disrupters, the innovators, the idea chasers.

Truth be told, I did my homework. I knew which teachers to put on *my radar. I heard about this spitfire of a teacher who I should get to know. I found myself visiting her classroom and quickly pushing her buttons to see what she was all about. I assumed she was thinking-- who the heck is this lady? Is she for real?*

I knew that Kristen was a forward-thinker who was looking to grow. I knew that she was waiting for an ally to advance students learning in new and exciting ways. I knew she was ready to be pushed, so I did.

I was smirking at her because I could feel her positive energy. My "look" was because I quickly knew that we would be on the same page. I smiled because I thought this girl is exactly the kind of teacher that I love as a leader. The kind who would take a gamble and say: Yes, I'll try it!

On that day, Jacie was my spark! She believed in me. She trusted me. She has continued to build trust with me, and in turn, we now ignite the passion in our students, continue to build confidence, and are getting out of the way.

As a teacher, I had to recognize that placing blame on my administration was becoming an excuse for me. It had become my go-to response when I faced difficult times and ideas that were turned away. In place of helping to fix the problem, I was allowing myself to become the problem. Disrupting education is not an easy process, and for me, innovation was not either. I had to choose this path for myself.

Have you been at these crossroads before?

Have you become complacent or worse, disgruntled over the decisions that you viewed or placed out of your own control?

Feeling lucky to have had someone believe in me was, without a doubt, a gift, but even more, I found a way to create my own luck and fortune through personal choices and actions.

 JACKPOT!

Opportunity is always out there; you simply need to see it and take the chance. What is the worst that could happen, you fail? No, actually, the worst thing to happen is to not take the chance at all. A single opportunity may surface in a student, a teacher, an administrator, parent, or community as a whole... be sure to pull the lever one more time!

DOUBLE DOWN

Going "All In" starts with one chance.

- What is one chance you are willing to take to lead to a better relationship with your students, admin, colleagues, or parents?
- What is one thing you can throw out of your teaching to create a better relationship between your students and learning?

ANTE UP with Rae Hughart

There have been multiple times in my life when I have felt lucky. Some of these memories stem from moments of a solution to a dilemma finally coming to fruition. Many are sparked from student success stories, and others live within the moments of learning. However, a memory of luck I always hold close to my heart was one I vividly remember having in my youth.

Growing up in an affluent area and struggling with an LD IEP diagnosis—seeing C's and D's year-after-year on report cards, it seemed each conversation in high school centered around the topic of not being accepted into college.

On a Saturday morning after taking a ballet class, LaVerne Lehman, my dance teacher, approached me about the opportunity to teach a dance class over the summer. Baffled by her request, I questioned why in the world she felt I would be a good fit for that opportunity. She looked at me puzzled, as only a stern dance instructor could, and said, "Because I believe in you."

This was the moment that changed my life. It carved my pathway into discovering my passion for teaching.

A teacher identifying characteristics in myself I was not even aware I possessed has had an everlasting impact —

not only on myself but on the thousands of students I have had the pleasure to serve.

- Rae Hughart, Director of Training for the Teach Better Team, 6th Grade Math Teacher in Normal, Illinois
- Follow on Twitter @RaeHughart

BET 6: ROLLING THE DICE

The Pit Boss Perspective

*H*ave you heard the roar that often erupts around the craps table? The dice are being thrown. The energy of the crowd is building. With each throw and subsequent win, the anticipation builds. You roll again. The crowd cheers. For some, it can become addicting.*

When you roll the dice in education and the gamble results in a small win, you inevitably keep coming back for more. The excitement of the win and the encouragement of the crowd push you to roll again. As leaders, when we encourage our teachers to roll the dice, we are giving them the freedom to take a chance. We are saying we trust you to make decisions as an educational professional.

It's not a trick. I'm not strategizing. I want you to take a gamble if it means that our students will benefit.

> **"As** administrators, when we encourage our teachers to roll the dice, we are giving them the freedom to take a chance and make a difference for our students"
>
> #ALLinEDU

By incorporating a novel into the classroom, an experience was created. I, too, created an experience. I met every child where they were at in their life. They love to dress up… so on that day, I did too! With overalls on, boots borrowed from my teenage son, and a lantern in my hand, I stood at the door waiting for my students to arrive. I was no longer trying to hide this experience and keep it all to myself so that I could fit it in without backlash. I was sharing it with the world, or at least my hallway! The giggles could be heard as students turned the bend to enter the hallway. *Mrs. Nan, what are you doing? Mrs. Nan, what are we doing?* I had an iMovie trailer playing that I had created based off of the novel. I wanted the trailer to draw interest to the novel without them even knowing a book was related to the moment I was creating. Music was playing, and the sounds of excitement filled the room.

I read every single word in the best hillbilly accent I could muster. We all dressed up in our favorite character from the story. We created our own experiences along the way. Students chose to show their learning through Scratch, Canva, iMovie, Google Slides, and so much more. How is this possible? How could I meet them where they were at with their ideas and technology when this was a story based on the Great Depression, a time they knew nothing about?

SIMPLE... I focused on the standards. If the standard requires that my students understand the problem and solution, why would I limit my assessment to a multiple-choice question on a 10-point reading test? Why not a Canva poster showing two puzzle pieces where the problem is stated in one piece and then connected to the solution in another? That is what one student created. Why not use Scratch to code a picture of the dog being stuck in an icy river with the solution of an unbent lantern handle being coded to pull him out? That wasn't my idea. I didn't even know how to code, but my student did!

We ate the almighty treat of Horehound, a tasty candy from this particular era... not because it was a standard as you may have guessed, but it was a treat that the main character Billy loved and cherished each time his grandfather gave him a nickel sack's worth. We couldn't just stop with the original, though. Before I knew it, my students were on a major hunt for this candy. They had to have more. Watermelon, cherry, root beer, lemon, and many more were found and brought in... not because I asked for it, but because they fell in love with it! They didn't fall in love with this candy because it was the best they ever tried, but because of the experience created around it.

We jetted off to Makerspace and created our own bank to start saving our money for that one thing we just "needed" to get our hands-on. In the book, Billy used an old KC Baking Powder can that he found out the back of the house. One year, we challenged ourselves to recreate that can, but by the next year, new students came with new ideas, and we were challenging ourselves to create cans using only paper-based on ones we could find in our recycling bins today. Oh, they were amazing! We had Chef Boyardee, Green Beans, Pepsi, and Coke, to name a few. They then wrote about what they were saving for and why it was so important to them. They masterminded a plan and wrote down the steps that they would take to obtain their goal. The creation of the can was not a standard, but the basic writing skill was just that. Better yet, the magic in their writing came from the love they found in reading!

And then it came to an end. Six weeks flew by in a blink of an eye. The students could not wait to hear what was next. They were beyond thrilled that I was meeting them where they were at... where their passions ran deep. Where they could make choices in their learning and share their voice without feeling disrespectful. But the only answer I had came in a scope and sequence pacing chart that dictated what we taught and on what day we taught it. I told the class we would be heading back into the anthology. They sighed. More like groaned.

Why all this fuss I asked? Their reply, "It will be the same thing over and over for days. It will be boring! You are killing us, Mrs. Nan."

Killing you, really? From that point forward, it was termed "The Five-Day Death March." To them, "The Five-Day Death March" went something like this... OK, kids, let's open up to our **new story (that is for those of you who have never read it before).** We are about to read to self, read to someone, listen to, word work, write about, and then regurgitate all the facts after **five repetitive days of the same story.** The use of the Daily Five Approach is a powerful tool, and yes, I do use it to help build great readers in my classroom. But this can be done with guided reading and does not need to be the singular way of teaching skills that students must acquire as a whole class. In my experience, by teaching a story over and over at this particular level, students memorize the concepts, but cannot carry the skills into other facets of their work.

Monday-Friday... left, right, left, ...

The weekly reading story that was pulled from the Anthology . . . the one attempting to serve all students of all abilities and passions, as the one and only focus on **reading.** This went on for five solid days for years and years and years. Did I mention that there will only be five questions on the predetermined assessment? They are super similar to what we have reviewed and discussed in length over the last *five days*. Let's not forget the eight vocabulary words that you may already know, but I still need to see if you can pick out the definition from four options. No worries... I won't ask you to put them into context. Just memorize the meaning, and you will be fine (DOK 1). Oh, then I'm going to give you a cold read to show that you now know how to use all the skills that you **didn't need to master** in order to **memorize** the story. I know you practiced them on a worksheet and excelled, but I have to say that **I am a little concerned you can't carry that over into other work.** Drum roll, please... Take home the GRADE!

Don't get me wrong, there is a need for repetition to build skills at all levels, but I was doing that each and every day with

Guided Reading and Daily Five (Read to Self, Read to Others, Listen to Reading, Word Work, and Writing). I truly believe that in order to teach skills, you must create a need for skills. It is simply based on relevance, and that becomes key when reaching all learners. I am not talking about reaching the majority of learners... I am talking about all of them! All or nothing, and I was ALL IN!

I had to do it... I had to go back to the boss and ask for more. I am my students' voice, right? That is how I saw it then, but oh, how times have changed. What more could I ask for? Where could I go with this? The sad truth is, I had not grown in so long that all I could think to do was ask for another novel study. How does that happen? How did I let myself go? When did it become okay to stop learning? (This is the point to which I wanted to send apology letters to every child this mindset may have negatively affected.)

So, I rolled the dice. Permission granted! This had my attention. If it was this simple to change just a couple of things, what more could I do?

JACKPOT!

Learning and growing as an educator means that we need to continue rolling the dice. Stop counting the attempts that didn't work and move forward. You never know when the next roll may be the winning one!

DOUBLE DOWN

- Try a new app or share one with a colleague.
- Co-plan a lesson with another teacher.
- Identify one instructional area for which you can roll the dice this week.
- Reach out to someone who can connect with your class. What can you plan? How might it positively impact your students?

ANTE UP with Maureen Hayes

Thomas C. Murray says, "Every time we fail, it's an opportunity to model how to get up and keep trying, to those that look to us for direction."

As educators, we continually encourage our students to take risks in the classroom as part of their learning journey. Children learn by example, and the more risks we model for students, the more we not only encourage but develop a climate where risks are expected and the process is celebrated.

As an educational leader, taking risks is part of my job.

If my goal as an effective leader is to meet the needs of students, taking risks and sharing my journey with staff is something I need to model. It is imperative that I am also transparent in sharing my barriers along with my successes as part of the risk-taking process. Our society instills in us the belief that failure is bad, but what we need to put the focus on is what we learn through the obstacles we face.

Brene Brown reminds us that we must be "in the arena" if we are to provide any meaningful support or feedback to others. I support risk-taking by standing shoulder-to-shoulder with staff in the classroom, modeling lessons, and working with students. It is crucial that I develop potential in staff through relationships and classroom visits that do not involve evaluation.

My goal is to demonstrate vulnerability as I establish a culture for risk-taking. Teachers need to know risks are not only encouraged, but will be supported and not punitive in the teacher evaluation process. This builds a positive momentum in any setting, leading towards more risk-taking and greater learning that has real-life applications for success. It's through risk-taking that goals can be met, discoveries made, and our greatest achievements are realized.

• Maureen Hayes, Elementary Humanities Supervisor in Lawrenceville, New Jersey
• Follow on Twitter @mhayes611

BET 7: PULL THE LEVER

What more did I want to do? Once again, why was I stuck in a zone of not knowing what I wanted for my students? Why had I lost sight of what I wanted for myself? Where had my voice gone? Was I afraid to share, or did I not have anything more to share? This simply had to change! I needed to reflect on my practice. I had to break down what was going right and what was terribly wrong. This could not be based solely on how I felt, but a true reflection of my students, their view on education, and their growth.

Truth be told, I thought I was giving my best and my best was not good enough for every child. My best was old and stagnant. My best was always wrapped in love and understanding, but it was not enough to reach every child as a learner. I had grown tired from defeat, and it showed in my approach to teaching. I was simply getting by and didn't even know it, or did I?

In the previous ten years, opportunities weren't given to

develop myself and grow within my profession, and I was no longer looking to give away my time to find it. No longer could I venture out of my district to view new ideas, let alone take the time to step into another colleague's classroom. Common planning time started to disappear, and heading to a conference was not up for conversation. The countless hours I had spent masterminding moments of impact that were turned down, some without even a simple conversation, had defeated me. Budgets were cut. Many times, orders that were created months in advance were cut without notice. Materials required to successfully execute lessons were no longer being furnished. The wait would continue, hoping that some items would soon arrive, and they simply did not come. I would pull the lever and invest in my students' time and time again because I knew they were worth every cent I spent. The out-of-pocket expense was no longer acknowledged, but more so expected, and it was building resentment inside of me.

Rarely do I hear an educator talk about the hours they devote to a lesson, let alone a unit. Why is that? Is it simply expected? Do we chalk it up to choice? What about the lessons that must come from the manual and must be taught the same as your colleagues? This is when I would find myself once again leaning into professional compliance and in turn, further away from growth.

I was spending time, money, and energy that seemed to go unnoticed. Do I pull the lever again or not?

You are Brave

You are a Risk Taker

You are Confident

YOU are ALL In

#ALLinEDU

The Pit Boss Perspective

Are we neglecting to see the whole picture here? Many factors go into a positive classroom experience. There are a lot of expectations that administrators have for classroom teachers. We want teachers to have a love for our students. We want to hug and high five them and build them up as caring people. We need teachers who will set clear expectations and provide boundaries, too. This requires teachers leading with their hearts. But we cannot just teach from the heart alone.

Our students also need teachers who will help them to learn, helping to build their brainpower and preparing them for the next grade level. Teachers who lead with the brain create reliable learning environments for students and focus on the content that is needed. This is an important factor, but we cannot just focus on the brain either because, in turn, we may neglect the other pieces.

One area that often gets overlooked is the future. Sometimes we are so stuck in the moment, teaching this one skill or working through one student's struggle that we lose sight of the opportunity to grow. We need to keep our minds focused on the here and now, but always have our eyes looking ahead to what is to come, preparing our students for an unknown future of possibilities.

Educating our students requires all of these factors to align, like the reels in a slot machine, to hit the jackpot. We may lose sight of ourselves as educators when we focus on one reel and neglect the others. Don't get me wrong. There are great teachers who focus on kindness and character education, but if they neglect the academic reel, then our students don't win. If we only focus on academics and not on the opportunity to grow, we miss the pay-off again. When all three reels (heart, mind, and future) align, our teachers are effective, and our students are successful.

JACKPOT!

When all three reels (heart, mind, and future) align, everyone is successful. Everyone has their strengths, but without nurturing and realigning our weaknesses, we cannot hit the jackpot! Everyone must be growing to move forward. This includes the administration, teachers, staff, students, parents, and community.

DOUBLE DOWN

Reflect on your strengths and hone in on your weaknesses.

- Do you lead with your heart or your mind?
- Do you provide a focus on the future?
- How can you ensure that all three factors are a part of your daily practice?

ANTE UP with Nicole Parrish

Technology is the way of the world. Many children start using technology at such a young age. Their technology experience is second nature by the time they enter elementary school. It only fits that more technology should be used in the classroom. I want to grow in this area. I want to know more about how to implement more technology into my classroom lessons. Using and implementing more technology would benefit my students and enrich the lesson overall. Technology is always changing and improving. I do not know everything that is out there to enhance my students' learning. In order to make this happen, I must seek out information on what is new for technology integration in schools. I can do this by reading educational books, magazines, blogs, and social media accounts. I need to jump at opportunities to go to training and professional development classes about technology integration. I want to collaborate more with my co-teachers and colleagues in my district. I should not be afraid to try something new in the classroom, even when I do not know much about it or have never used it before. I need to use the new opportunity as a teaching moment for my students and me, that we're all going to learn something new together.

- Nicole Parrish, Elementary Teacher in Hopewell Area School District, Pennsylvania
- Follow on Twitter @parrishn18

ANTE UP with Anna Kostrick

Growth. There isn't a student meeting that goes by without the mention of that word. Can you prove growth? How much growth has the student had? What are the barriers to growth? Within all of these discussions, it's not often that I am being pushed by others to reevaluate my own growth. What do I need to do to grow as an educator? What growing could I do that would impact my students most? These questions are heavy and hard. Parents. Community. Outside resources.

Shiver. These things make me nervous. I try to be a rock-star educator. I love my students hard. I go to bat for them however I can, but I DREAD having to call parents or send emails. I get nervous at the thought of working outside of my building to create partnerships that would benefit my students. What if my ideas are stupid? What if I can't prove that what I'm doing will be successful? What if it isn't successful?

It is okay if my students watch a lesson go bad because I use that as a teachable moment about perseverance, growth, and failing forward. But then I wonder if there are more stakeholders watching, what will they think of me? Will they support me in my next endeavor?

I know that my next steps need to involve community, parents, and outside resources to push my thinking and to give my students opportunities outside of what I can offer alone.

• Anna Kostrick, Elementary Teacher in Hopewell Area School District, Pennsylvania
• Follow on Twitter @MrsKTweets

BET 8: CASH IN ON OPPORTUNITY

*T*hen the email came. The one that announced **more opportunity**... a time commitment that mirrored a boot camp for teachers, but in the most exciting way! For the first time in my career, I was given a calendar of opportunities that would empower me (and my students) to move forward. I looked over the calendar and found areas of interest.

There were days set aside within the grade level. What was our vision? What did we want for our students? Was she looking for our opinion? Our voice? Would we all have to be on the same page? We ourselves are different... would that be embraced?

There were days set aside to talk about innovation. Honestly, at this point, I wasn't even sure what innovation looks like in the classroom. I could barely bring myself to the status quo, let alone innovative. Questions started rolling around in my mind.

Would I have anything to offer? Would I be on the outside looking in? Where do I fit into this picture?

There were days to talk about the future of the district. To talk about grants and how we could impact every child with the support of local businesses that are ready to project education forward.

There were days allotted for FIELD TRIPS!

There were days allotted to re-envision our curriculum. Yes, the term and definition of the curriculum were open for discussion. A term that has been improperly defined over and over.

How do you define curriculum? Is it something set for you or with you? Does it have room for change, or is it one more constant that your district continues to push out?

For years, we were brought together to map out the curriculum for our grade level. The part that left little to no room for envisioning that map was the directive to bring along the manuals purchased for each subject. We would then each take a manual and map out which chapters, units, and lessons would be taught on specific days and particular months. A copy was then dispersed to each grade level teacher. This was then added to the school framework in a computer system that we didn't access. Why? Because it was done, and there was never a thought that it would change in any way until we piloted something new in the years to come.

There was no opportunity to talk about the use of novels, videos, literature beyond the anthology, technology, passion projects, Genius Hour, or anything that would bring in sporadic, opinionated, and possibly isolated forms of growth beyond the publisher we had chosen for that particular subject. The manual was beyond a guide; it was a required constant by which we were monitored to ensure all students were receiving the same content as the next. In retrospect, this may have been an assumption on my part, but when you are told what to do and how to do it without an opportunity to discuss anything in between, you find yourself reacting with professional compliance even when you strongly disagree.

The Pit Boss Perspective

Sometimes we improperly define things in education because we don't know any better. Other times, it's because it is the way we've always done things. It can be hard to change that mindset and look at it in a new way. Have you been asked to come in for a curriculum writing meeting and told to copy information from your textbook and put it directly into a curriculum document? Teams are given a day (or even less) to input information into some online curriculum mapping program with little thought given to how or why. In your district, is "curriculum" synonymous with the teacher's manual? Is the curriculum a document that was written, put in a binder, and placed on a shelf? Is it a quick process for a select few to sit in a room, duplicate what is already in the manual with some standards tossed in? Or is it a meaningful, inclusive process that digs deep into what students should know and be able to do in the classroom?

That summer, we had a lot of hard work to do. We needed to talk about curriculum, instruction, and assessment. We had to dig in and define the way we were going to move forward as a district. It was a critical point as we took a new trajectory. We needed to look at the way we handled grants and figure out how to get more technology into the hands of our students. There was so much we needed to tackle. It required time and energy on the part of teachers and administrators, working together towards a common vision for the school district. It was an opportunity to create positive change.

❖

The only issue was that my areas of interest were broad and going to require a large chunk of my summer. This had now gone from exciting to scary. How would I make this happen? How would I find a way to balance being a mother and wife with my passion for being the best teacher I can possibly be? I wasn't even sure what I was looking for... I just knew I was looking for a change. Sign me up! I gave myself permission to take care of myself. To gain more knowledge that was being offered. To regain my confidence by educating myself. But let's face it, this decision was not my own to make.

Educators take an incredible amount of time from their families in ways many do not grasp, and this summer was no exception. I was not going to be able to squeeze this in during a family movie like correcting a stack of papers. I was not moving into a quiet territory to make another parent phone call after their child had gone to bed. I was not going to be taking a day away from them to wrap it all up in one fell swoop. No, I wasn't trying to squeeze my teaching time in... I was looking for radical change and large amounts of time. This meant going to my family and having a heart-to-heart talk.

I had a sit-down chat with them. All of them... my husband Eric, along with my sons Trent and Jack. This chat would be a true game-changer. They knew I had lost the spark that had naturally been lit for so long. For the first time in my career, I needed someone else to help me keep that fire burning, or I was considering leaving the profession **that I always believed was created just for me.** What had happened to me? Why did I feel so isolated? Why did I feel so defeated? Why was I the outcast in education... **or at least why did I feel that way?**

My family was ALL IN! But like most families, I realized that this was going to spill over into additional supports outside of my own home. This was a key moment because it was reflective as to why I was unable to open the door so many times before. This is why so many educators have to turn down a chance at growth. Why? Because "on their own time" isn't their own time. It is family time. It is husband time. Child time. Caring for family members. It is mental health. It is the extra job they work to create opportunities for their family time. It is time volunteered for their church, family, and community. It is priceless time that is given up to grow just to be stifled by the word, no.

As with most, we call on our extended family to carry us. I was no different. I called my mother-in-law and friend, the late Sandy Nan. Without her to care for the boys, and run them to sports, I was never going to be able to make the commitment that was necessary for change... the kind I was about to get with this incredible opportunity. Mom said, "absolutely!" without hesitation. Just like most, I, too, needed that one person to give me the extra shove. Not the guilt trip of taking time from my family, but the support of "go get it!" She was truly my biggest supporter. She was my biggest fan! She got me... she remembered when the fire burned inside of me. She herself devoted 52 years in education as the secretary of our junior high before retiring that very same year. Her one single passion was loving children. This opportunity was exactly what she wanted for me... for **our** children... for all children! She didn't just support me, she pushed me! She demanded that I take every opportunity that was coming my way and then share it with others.

The summer of 2016 was EPIC! I spent more time learning, creating, and being inspired than I did sitting poolside, and it was phenomenal! I was bonding with others in my district that were ready for change. Ready to be the change! Although I had been in the district for almost two decades at this point, I had never even had a conversation with half of my colleagues. Let the journey begin! The excitement was contagious! I started receiving texts from others, asking what this was all about. How could they get in? Was this real? Oh, this was real!

Teaching is such a challenging profession. It takes control, patience, balance, understanding, and so much more. We are limited on downtime and the recharging of our mental health during the school year, especially if we have kids of our own. We go from teacher to Mom and back again (for days) without breaks to slip away into our own space. Often we go days without breaks and do not get to slip away, ever. Relationships are personal and are exhausting. Why? Because they revolve around love. And we love our students. We don't flip a switch at 4:00 and call an end to our day even though we have our own families to take care of too. When working one-on-one with children, we need to be mindful of our own well-being. A role of an educator is different than many professions, and therefore our needs are too.

I found myself brainstorming again, and with a purpose! I felt I had a reason to be a teacher again... the kind that I knew every child deserved. Like my students, I am not cut from a mold, nor do I excel by being treated that way. I need to matter. I need to matter the way my students matter to me! I was up out of bed before my alarm went off. I was knocking down the door of the school to get in... to be amongst the goodness, the true force to education... I mattered again!

The Pit Boss Perspective

I began my administrative role in the district in mid-July, which is generally quiet in central office, but this was uncomfortably quiet. Nothing was happening! No professional learning was scheduled. Teachers weren't coming together to plan for the new year. No goals were being set. Conversations weren't occurring. No excitement was brewing. At that moment, I knew that I needed to take steps to plan for the following summer so that we could begin to change that trajectory.

Throughout the year, it became apparent that the teachers across our five school buildings weren't connected. They didn't even know each other. We are a district of about 2200 students and 200 educators, so it is not this enormous system, but yet people who taught there for 20 years didn't know other educators in the system.

How would I help educators to establish relationships with one another?

I planned an unconventional day of learning--a teacher field trip. I sent an invitation out to the entire district, not having any clue how many people would respond. Twenty-five showed up that morning (at least half of them just to see what this crazy, new assistant super was all about). Over coffee and donuts, one teacher pulled me aside and sadly said, "I don't know most of the people in this room." So, we introduced ourselves and started new connections that would later turn into cross-building collaborations.

We boarded a school bus and headed out for a day of fun and exploration together: teachers, principals, and administrators.

We visited some unique places in Pittsburgh, including the Center for Creative Reuse and Construction Junction. We ate lunch together and had informal conversations. Conversations that I was reminded "never happen with admin."

Our journey continued to Inventionland, a magical place of innovation that is like walking into Willy Wonka's Chocolate Factory. The teachers were excited. They were smiling. They were talking. The relationships were starting to form.

I had to create a way to invite teachers to build their skills.

During that first summer, we planned a series of professional learning opportunities that would pull teachers together to continue building those relationships, but also provide opportunities for them to build skills in different areas. We initiated an "innovation committee" and opened the conversation around what our schools could be. We held workshops around grant writing so that teachers would be equipped to fund the things that they needed for their classrooms. We engaged in curriculum work so that teachers could have meaningful conversations around effective teaching and learning. We offered opportunities to learn more about project-based learning through a local school district. Our calendar was full of opportunities that summer. More chances to connect. More conversations.

If this was going to grow into something bigger, we needed to give permission for teachers to innovate.

At every meeting that summer, I was intentional about giving teachers permission. Sometimes they need to hear that it is OK to try something new. No, there is no catch. I am not trying to play "gotcha." I gave teachers permission to connect with students, try new materials, and infuse technology--whatever it takes!

Oh, the smiles! That was how I was greeted each time I entered another day of learning. Was this really summer? Were these teachers for real? No moaning or groaning. This must not be Professional Development.

This, my friends, was about creating change. The excitement grew with each question asked. Each attempt at creating a new idea. I asked if I could and was told YES. I asked again, and again, and again. The response was YES.

Was this too good to be true? Was this a test? Was this to test my ability to make decisions, my willingness to take risks, or a test to see if I would fail? I am not a worrier by nature, but I had become hesitant to be the free spirit I was down deep. Each time I left my guard down in the past, I would find myself burnt. When was I going to learn? I felt the fear creep over me. The fear of a dream going bust. The fear of, *what if I try and it fails? What then?* Fortunately, my instinct to lean into joy and goodness was stronger than the fear that loomed in my mind. As the summer drew to a close, I felt like a new person, as if I had a new lease on life. Something had changed in me. For the first time since I had been hired, I felt believed in! I felt in control... empowered! I sat on my patio, letting the sun hit my face when my son Trent came to my side, holding the mail...

JACKPOT!

Opportunities are all around. Sometimes they are bold opportunities to take, and other times you need to seek them out. Whether it is a book with a new perspective, a blog to read, a podcast to listen to, a Twitter chat to jump in, or a simple conversation with someone outside of your normal "go-to" circle, a new perspective awaits!

DOUBLE DOWN

- Teachers--how can you cash in on opportunities for students?
- Administrators--what opportunities can you create for teachers to unleash their imagination?

ANTE UP with Hans Appel

As educators, the decisions we make have real life-changing outcomes for our students. Several years ago,

I found myself at a precipice of opportunity when someone with a mentorship request looked to do his school counseling internship with me. Having an intern forces one to take a deep dive into relooking at everything we do. With fresh, open eyes, interns can often unintentionally cast light on outdated procedures, programs, and/or practices. Their very presence initiates the kind of necessary introspection that often gets pushed to the side, in favor of mandates, routines, and requirements. Indeed, my willingness to take on a mentee (Nate) almost guaranteed my educational growth and forever set me on a path towards the intentional pursuit of an award-winning culture.

My time with Nate allowed me to see a pressing need to revamp our social-emotional learning program, PBIS (Positive Behavior Interventions and Supports) efforts, and perhaps most importantly our school's communication and connection beyond the four walls of Enterprise Middle School. Thanks to the inherent reflective practices in educational mentorship, I discovered incredible programs like Character Strong and PBIS Rewards to bring a positive shockwave into our school's ecosystem. These whole child programs coupled with ongoing support from educational trainers like John Norlin and Houston Kraft helped us put an intentional servant leadership framework around our relationship-driven focus at EMS. And our rebranding to Wildcat Nation through a specific school-wide emphasis of Character, Excellence, and Community directly led to a host of educational awards and recognitions, including: 2018

ASCD Whole Child Award in Washington State, 2018
Global Class Act Award for Kindness, and 2019 PBIS
Film Festival Finalist (while taking top prize in the
Parents, Staff, Community Category).

As our school continued to gain local, regional and
national attention, I was compelled to further develop
my PLN through blogging, presenting, and connecting. These OPPORTUNITIES ultimately led my wife,
Jennifer, and I to take a group of leadership students
to an inspirational SERVUS (SERVE and US) leadership conference (learn more about SERVUS here:
servusconference.com/aboutservus). During the
conference, we had the epiphany to surround our
students with exceptional leaders through a new innovative learning platform. Additionally, we searched for
a way to share these learnings, reflections, and
moments with an authentic audience. These discussions led us to our current quest to amplify student
voice through student-led podcasting and video development which have subsequently morphed into
incredible passion project-based learning such as
Award Winning Culture and AWC-tv. My decision to
venture into mentorship has had a game-changing
impact on our students, community, and K-12 education around the world. My mentorship journey is a
wonderful reminder that when we cash in on life's
opportunities and willingly lean-in to professional
risk-taking, we have the chance to forever shatter the
ceiling on student voice!

- Hans Appel, Creator of "Award Winning Culture", Counselor in West Richland, WA
- Follow on Twitter @awculture

ANTE UP with Sam Fecich

I prepare future teachers in the areas of educational technology and special education. To keep on my "A" game, I tune into Twitter, Instagram, and podcasts and stay up-to-date and current with methods and technology tools that can impact and engage learners. Not only can I bring this information back to my classroom through hands-on activities, but I can also direct my students to this information through sharing it on social media with our department hashtag #GCCEDU.

I have had many opportunities present themselves through being a connected teacher. One of my most valuable opportunities is being a lead on the ISTE Teacher Education Network (TEN) where I work with higher education leaders and current educators on a monthly basis to discuss how we can make a difference in preparing future teachers. Through this connection, I was able to lead an event that we do each year during ISTE – our pre-conference, which is a free professional development opportunity for preservice teachers, current teachers, and higher ed professionals to learn, lead and connect.

I learned all about Edcamps by being a connected

educator. One day I was bebopping around Twitter and I saw a free professional development event at a neighboring school – it was called an EdCamp. I had no idea what it was, but it was free and my preservice teachers can afford FREE! I took four preservice teachers with me and we traveled to our first Edcamp. We learned so much that day but beyond discussions, we connected with other educators. From there we brought back the idea of an Edcamp to Grove City College where we just finished our fourth yearly Edcamp that has been developed, created, and run by preservice teachers.

One final opportunity that I made through my professional learning network was ECET2, which is a national convening sponsored by the Bill and Melinda Gates Foundation. I learned about it online through a connection and was accepted to attend a convening in New Jersey with two colleagues and two preservice teachers. We presented about digital portfolios and the power of being connected. It was fantastic to have preservice teachers join in on the presentation and show that they have a voice in education. Since then I have attended one other ECET2 and co-led an ECET2 designed for preservice teachers in April 2019 where 100 future educators from North West PA came to learn from leaders in the field and network.

Friends, not all opportunities are going to pan out and that is OK. Trust me, there will be more. What is important is to find opportunities that speak to you and that will grow you as an educator and leader. They are out there – just take the first step and get connected!

• Dr. Sam Fecich, Professor at Grove City College, Pennsylvania, Author of EduMagic
• Follow on Twitter @SFecich

BET 9: TOKEN OF APPRECIATION

*A*s my son Trent was returning from the mailbox, I could see that a small envelope had gotten his attention and left him with a quizzical look on his face. I asked him what was on his mind, and he said there was a card addressed to him, his brother Jack, and his dad. I immediately told him to open it. The suspense would kill us to wait for my husband to get home. So, we did. It was a card from Jacie to my family. I could barely read it. The tears rolled down my face. Trent put his arm around me and asked if he could finish reading it for me. Jacie was thanking my family. She was thanking them for sacrificing their family time with me so that I could grow. So that I could be the best teacher I could possibly be. She was **thanking my family.** I picked up the phone and called my mother-in-law. I couldn't get the words out through my tears. She could tell they were tears full of so much emotion.

Tears of joy

Tears of redemption

Tears of gratefulness

Tears of appreciation

Tears of pain

The pain, I needed to let go of so that I could fully embrace the pure goodness to which I had right there in my life. Mom knew what this meant to me. She knew that this was all I needed to continue my journey. To move mountains again. To knock down barriers in education. To be my own voice and own it. To be prideful. To be a change agent for all children! My last words that day on the phone were, "Mom, I wish you could have worked for her. You would have loved her." Mom's reply was, "I do."

> **"T**he words **thank you** changed the entire **trajectory** of **learning** for my students and me."
>
> #ALLinEDU

The Pit Boss Perspective

The truth is, I wrote a lot of cards that initial summer. I wrote cards to individuals who stepped out of their comfort zones and attended our teacher field trip. They needed to know that their risk-taking was appreciated. I wrote cards to the husbands and wives of our princi-

pals who were working long hours and spending time away from home. Families are an important part of our success as a district. The families of our administrators needed to understand that we valued the sacrifice that is made in education.

I wrote cards to teachers who used what they learned at our grant-writing workshop to secure funding for new projects. Celebrating their success was so important. I wrote cards to the families of teachers who took advantage of every opportunity that I offered that summer. We needed to make sure that the spouses and children of our teachers know that we appreciate their support. I took special care in my letter to Kristen because I knew that it would be as special to her as it was to me.

The token of appreciation goes both ways. I was out of the office for a meeting in another building when I returned and found a gift on my desk. It was a desk-size gumball machine filled with M&Ms. Now I love me some chocolate, but these weren't your average M&Ms. This nut (Kristen) went and made customized candies with my face on them! Insane, right? Since the superintendent and I both have last names starting with Ms., the candy was quite appropriate. In addition to our faces, the candy also had motivational words and phrases on them.

At first, I cracked up, laughing at this. After all, it is quite strange seeing your face on a candy that you are now consuming. But once it all sunk in, I became extremely emotional. Not only had I impacted this teacher, but she actually took the time to come up with a gift that was so very personalized. The candy machine sits on my desk as a constant reminder that I need to take the time to connect with teachers and nurture the relationships that can make our schools even stronger.

The token of appreciation can be as simple as a note or a sticker or as elaborate as a gift as long as it comes from the heart. Recognizing those in your school community for the work they are doing is a huge step towards building relationships and creating a momentum for positive change.

JACKPOT!

Take time to appreciate those who matter. These can be small, thoughtful gestures to connect that truly make a difference.

DOUBLE DOWN

- How will you provide a token of appreciation to the people who are making a difference in your school?
- Send a note of thanks to an administrator, teacher, staff member, student, parent, and or member of the community.
- Go "ALL IN" and send a note of thanks to each one!

ANTE UP with Roman Nowak

"Gratitude can transform common days into thanksgivings, turn routine jobs into joy, and change ordinary opportunities into blessings." — *William Arthur Ward*

The most important calling we have as people is sharing our appreciation and gratitude with those around us. As educators, if we lead and teach with our hearts, we will inspire students, colleagues, and community members to always make a difference in the world. Similarly to kindness and hope, if we make gratitude a foundational element of our daily lives and mission, it will, in turn, become a priority and we will allow the necessary time for it. It is important to be authentic and purposeful in planning out our acts of gratitude.

As a father and teacher, I strive to be a role model for my daughters and my students. In doing so, I try to plan out specific moments on a regular basis where I share my appreciation for others. Often times, in the spirit of random acts of kindness, I leave these actions anonymous, so that those whom I celebrate can simply relish in the celebration. I also aspire to be as creative as possible in the chosen actions so that the people I interact with feel unique and special. Before the 2019-2020 school year began, I wanted to share my upcoming appreciation for each of my students and the time we would spend together. I took the time to prepare a letter and a poem that I mailed out to each student and when they arrived to class, I had a special token waiting for them. A card and a pack of Excel gum that read: "Welcome *name of student*, Hope you are ready to EXCEL this semester! Mr. Nowak". It is the small gestures that are often appreciated the most by others. It is important to embrace these moments and capitalize on them to raise the souls of others.

I have also been blessed to be on the receiving end of some special tokens of appreciation. When you share positivity and kindness with the world, oftentimes it will come back to you in the most unexpected ways. From t-shirts to care packages and letters, there have been many experiences that I hold dear to my heart. The most remarkable gift and token of appreciation has been from a Grade 1 class in Auburndale, Florida. After connecting with Ms. Miller's class at Caldwell Elementary, sharing stories and kindness challenges, the students wrote and put together a Kindness Book in my honor. We may often take the time to share the words *Thank You* with those around us, but it is the actions and the unique gestures that truly leave an imprint on the heart of others and create the greatest impact.

• Roman Nowak, High School Teacher in Ontario, Canada
• Follow on Twitter @NowakRo

BET 10: MILLION DOLLAR DECISION

*W*ith the excitement of change unfolding, so was the talk among teachers.

What is <u>she</u> doing now?

How is <u>she</u> allowed to do that?

Is this acceptable?

Who does <u>she</u> think she is?

I heard from earshot... but not in reference to me, to Jacie. **Do you think she is going to hire the people we want?** Yes, the talk of hiring. The investment we each have in our people. One has to ask, is it an emotional investment with an isolated return, or is this the jackpot... the one that tilts the world and takes it for a spin?

I ended up overhearing a conversation with Jacie and the hiring process. I, too, was invested in a handful of people that I wanted to see hired. I wanted to know what *she* was looking for in a new hire, so I listened in. She said it very simple and matter of fact, "When I hire, I hire the best. Each new teacher is a Million Dollar Decision!"

The Pit Boss Perspective

I remember that morning after a late night of interviewing. Teachers were settling in for a professional development session that I was leading. I knew that a few teachers were really advocating for a particular candidate to be hired. I knew there was a chance that they were going to push a bit about whether the committee had decided for an open position. Did they realize the weight of such a decision? This wasn't a small bet. This was like pushing all the chips onto your lucky number and spinning the roulette wheel with all your might.

Hiring a teacher is one of the most important things we get to do as a school system. We decide who is going to greet our students every day. We decide who is going to teach your son how to read. We decide who is going to counsel your middle schooler when things get tough. We decide who is going to motivate your child to want to come to school every day. I can't, in good conscience, make that decision based on who someone is friends with. I can't endorse someone just because they are your neighbor's babysitter or your cousin's mailman's wife. We are talking about the individual who is going to care for our kids.

And not just in their first year. Or until they have tenure. I want the person who will still be giving everything they've got 10, 20 years from now. The decision to hire someone, the right person, is a million-dollar decision. I am looking for that person to nurture, excite, and teach our students potentially for the next 30 years. Truly, that's over a million dollars, so I don't take these decisions lightly.

Interviewing potential new teachers is one of the most important parts of my job. I do take an unconventional approach to the interview process. You see, I don't really care what your GPA was in college. I'm not highly impressed by which university you attended. Can you believe I once had a board member tell our committee that just because a candidate went to Notre Dame that we should hire her for a teaching position? Now, I don't have anything against Notre Dame (or any other school for that matter). I am sure that their graduates are highly educated, but this individual was not the right fit for this position. She did not provide full answers to the interview questions, and her model lesson was average at best--but she went to Notre Dame.

I always ask questions that are a little off the beaten path, too. I don't care if you know all the steps of Madeline Hunter's lesson design. I don't need to know if you know what acronyms (IEP, ESSA, PSAT) stand for. I want to get at what you are like as a person and how you push yourself to be a stronger educator.

I often ask what teaching candidates are currently reading to determine whether they are up-to-date with current books and blogs. I ask them what their digital footprint says about them. Are they on Twitter? Can I look them up? And I usually do, right there in the interview. I want to know if they post relevant content from their classrooms or share relevant educational articles.

I ask if they blog or if they're active on Instagram. These things tell me what they will be like when they are teachers in our schools. You see, I want teachers who will be connected educators, who will tell their story, our story. I want teachers who keep up to date with what is happening education, who know what is relevant, and understand that education is in a constant state of change. We need teachers who *are agile enough to change with it. I don't want teachers who know everything. I want teachers who are willing to learn and grow personally. You can't always tell that from reading someone's resume.*

An interview should be like a conversation, not a firing squad. It should be a way to get to know an individual, their background, their likes and dislikes, the path that brought them to education. The teachers I've hired, they're passionate, interesting, smart, and funny. I guess that's "my type." I've learned over time that those are ultimately the people who make the best teachers. They know that connecting with people is important. They know that laughing should be a part of every day. They know that teaching is more about relationships than it is about anything else.

While we may take a gamble on a wild card candidate once in a while, I am always looking for the BEST person for the job, for our schools and our students. Are you worth the next million?

Mic drop! A Million Dollar Decision. Was I? I mean, would I still be? I started to self-reflect. I was questioning, had I done enough to be better? I felt horrible. She hadn't hired me... would she if she could? This was a whole new perspective. She didn't get to pick me just like I didn't get to pick her. Or how our students don't get to pick us. I left that day wondering. I left curious.

This led to a conversation to which Jacie asked me what I was reading. What was I reading? I didn't have time to read. I was changing the world on a whole different level! Not! Sigh! This is when I put myself in check. I heard hype around a book called

The Innovator's Mindset: Empower Learning, Unleash Talent, and Lead a Culture of Creativity, written by George Couros. I grabbed it off of Amazon and had it in my hands the next day. Oh, I had it, but I didn't open it just yet. I was never an avid reader, so this looked like a chore to me at first. Truth is, if it wasn't for the strong desire to be able to engage in conversation about "a book" I have read, I am not sure that I would have even opened it.

Then it happened... WOW! What a powerful moment! Was this really reading? I felt like I was on the phone with a friend, and they were speaking my language. I couldn't put it down. I read and googled to learn more about him and his teaching background. George shared his life with each of us as readers. He brought us into his world and invited us to know his parents. He shared their work ethic, their sacrifices, their words of wisdom. Then he said, "CHANGE is an OPPORTUNITY to do SOMETHING AMAZING" (Couros, 2015, p. 2). I felt these words in my core. **Yes, George,** I said... **it is!** George and I were having a conversation, and he didn't even know it. A book had never spoken to me like this before.

The Pit Boss Perspective

George's book is transformational for teachers and leaders. It provides insight and encouragement. For me, it provided critical reminders as I was in a role that meant I was a change agent. Change for some teachers may be a bad word. George reminds us that what people hear when we talk about change it that their current practice is not good enough. That they aren't working hard enough or that they are doing something wrong. I catch myself pushing initiatives and forget-

ting to reflect on this. As administrators, we need to stop and ask ourselves how we are approaching and supporting new initiatives. How do the teachers feel about this change? Am I projecting that they are doing something incorrectly? How can I reframe this work to emphasize the importance of growth and improvement?

It is easy to come in as a leader and see things from only the Pit Boss's perspective. School and district admin know this. We want to fix things. We want to lead. We want our schools and districts moving forward. But we can't get there if we don't have teachers who are ready to innovate and willing to learn and grow together. Change will simply never happen unless you have the courage to roll the dice and build the necessary relationships in your schools.

 **JACKPOT!**

Whether you are a new hire, a seasoned educator, or nearing retirement, BE THE MILLION DOLLAR DECISION for every child! Never settle, the risk is in the willing, and the willing changes lives one relationship at a time.

DOUBLE DOWN

- **What is one thing that you can do to ensure you are the best hire?**

- In what area of your practice do you feel you are most innovative?
- What area of practice do you want to push yourself for growth?

ANTE UP with Amy Burch

We approach the hiring process as a team and intentionally design the process to identify highly-qualified teachers that will fit the innovative culture we have worked so hard to create. Our approach decreases the gamble of introducing a new teacher to our culture. Candidates' first introduction to a school district is the cover letter and application. It is critical that candidates take the time to ensure the information is accurate and grammatically correct. Our team reads and highlights key terms in candidates' cover letters and resumes. Earning a face-to-face interview provides the candidates the opportunity to demonstrate a positive attitude and enthusiasm for the teaching profession. We identify candidates who demonstrate excellent communication skills, both verbal and written. Candidates must be able to use various methods of communication to meet the needs of students, parents, administrators, and colleagues. We evaluate candidates' knowledge of subject matter by requiring them to create a lesson to be taught. Designing a lesson that incorporates their knowledge into real-world situations is a strong indicator that student engagement will be high. Our goal is to hire teachers who value the inquiry of students, so questioning techniques are also evaluated. Student input is gathered through lesson observation and direct questioning. Sometimes the final characteristic that separates one candidate from another is the commitment to professional development. When investing over a million dollars into a teacher (*approximately a 30-year career that is*), we are looking for the complete package; positive, enthusiastic, effective communicator, knowledgeable, engaging, and committed to professional development.

• Dr. Amy M. Burch, Superintendent in Pittsburgh, Pennsylvania
• Follow on Twitter @AmyMBurchDEd

BET 11: IT'S ALL ABOUT THE VIEW

*I*nnovation vs. Iteration? I never thought about it. I **need to think about it!** Then I read this,

> " Being a teacher is not a superpower; the way we teach is. It's the mindset that you bring into the classroom and to the school that can help change the world." —George Couros (Couros, 2015, p. 227)

Once again, George was speaking my language. I went back to look at the eight characteristics again. Where did I fit into all of this? Where were my strengths and weaknesses? I no longer had to force myself to reflect, I was yearning to! As per George (Couros, 2015, p.48), an "innovator's mindset" is:

1. Empathetic
2. A Problem Finder
3. A Risk-Taker

4. Networked
5. Observant
6. A Creator
7. Resilient
8. Reflective

I focused in on number five, observant. Do we, as educators, take time to observe? I can't help but think we put a lot of pressure on ourselves to know the answers to most everything we are asked. Think about the first time you meet a child's parents a mere two weeks into school at the annual Open House. What is the first thing they are compelled to ask...? How is my child doing? That is a loaded question that comes with an incredible amount of responsibility. If you answer with "great," that may mislead the parents into thinking that everything is just fine when there may be concerns. If you answer with, "okay" that opens the door to questions and a very awkward moment. Let's not even go to "not as well as I would like" because that simply shouldn't exist in the first couple weeks of school, right? What is so bad about saying, I am still observing your child and getting to know them... let me tell you about #ObserveMe and how that impacts both my students and me. Why not open the door for an innovative approach that could benefit their child and remove our need to know everything?

Observing can lead to amazing things, including the characteristics of an Innovator's Mindset. Isn't that why **facilitating** is becoming the **new teaching**? As I continued to read another chapter in the book, I sat and listed what "observing" would give an educator and in turn, every child:

1. A New Perspective: How do they solve problems without me? **Do they need me**, and how much? If I am always posing the problem, will they ever truly be able to solve it? What about a scenario? Can they see the problem themselves without me? Tossing out an idea, a skill, a concept, or an event will allow me to observe their strengths and weaknesses so that I can, in turn, plan my next move.

2. Individualized Goals: What do they need versus what do I want to give? Is learning really about a pacing chart or a map? I have students in a class that were born at the same time others were crawling or even walking... all in one class! Do you know how many milestones a baby has in their first year of life? What on earth would I be doing right if I thought each of my learners was on the same "growth page"? Did one baby wait for another to crawl or before they were allowed to walk? Each student must have goals that are focused on their own individual growth.

3. Empathy: Who are the students from the inside out? How do they show this to others, and what does that tell me about them? Observing a child's reaction to a situation can speak volumes. It is a map of their life experiences. Are they able to have empathy? Are they able to infer what is happening for others at that moment? Can they truly put themselves in the other person's shoes?

I am observant. I notice the smallest details. The positive. The mindset of all. My journey continues, and by observing, I will learn... not for a moment, a day, or a week. I will learn for a lifetime. It came time for me to close the book for the day, and I needed a bookmark to hold my page. Quick and without thinking, I saw a dollar on the counter and grabbed it. As I stuck the dollar in the book, I realized what a perfect reminder it was for me... a million-dollar reminder!

"Embracing the possibilities is lifelong learning."

#ALLinEDU

The Pit Boss Perspective

And she is. Kristen is an investment that I would make again because while others walked away disgruntled that their neighbor, friend, or hairdresser's niece wasn't hired, she walked away, remembering the importance of that decision. She thought about the magnitude of the decision to hire an educator. As an administrator, I think carefully about every decision because I am recommending a candidate for a lifetime role as the teacher of our students. Consider the gravity of that decision. Kristen did. She pushes herself every day to demonstrate her abilities so that we are confidently renewing in that bet to hire her time and time again.

Of the eight characteristics of an Innovator's Mindset, I've spent the last two years focusing on being networked. The power of a learning network can propel you forward as an educator. I used one opportunity to create a network that could support innovation in our county. With grant funding, we connected three area school districts to estab-

lish the Beaver County Innovation and Learning Consortium. Not only does this network meet face-to-face, but we also extended the learning through social media tools like Twitter and Voxer to stay connected. We have worked to expand collaboration across traditional boundaries and make a difference in every classroom. Find out what we're up to on Twitter:

@BeaverCountyILC

In the first cohort of teacher leaders (we are now working on Cohort 3!), we chose to read Innovator's Mindset for a professional book study. We would read a chapter or two each week, and then I would post questions on Voxer for everyone to respond to. It was a way for our cohort to stay connected in between our monthly face-to-face meetings.

Voxer was a risk for some in our cohort. Nervous to share their story or to even hear their own voice, some teachers were reluctant to participate. I tried to serve as a model and support their learning. Slowly but surely, the team would chime in, sharing insight into what innovation looks like in their classrooms or which of the eight characteristics they felt were a strength. While Voxer was an uncomfortable stretch for some, it allowed the teachers to learn from other perspectives, providing a different view. We were able to use technology as a tool to enhance our collaboration and continue to build bridges across our county while strengthening our own educational practices.

Prior to our work within this consortium, our view was limited. We used this opportunity to not only break down barriers between teachers and administrators, but we also eliminated barriers among neighboring districts. Our teams made connections that led them to visit schools and collaborate with teachers in other school districts.

Some educators leveraged this initial opportunity into the chance to present at the local and state level, expanding their view even further and looking at what was possible beyond what they previously considered.

JACKPOT!

Being an observant and connected educator increases our awareness of the great things happening in education. These characteristics can fuel us to be better and learn more.

DOUBLE DOWN

- Who have you observed lately?
- What is one take away from that observation that you could take back in your classroom to make a change for the better?
- When reflecting on your own voice, how do you share it with others?
- How do you create an opportunity for others to share with you?

ANTE UP with Mandy Froehlich

For a long time, as I worked on developing myself as an educator, I felt like there couldn't possibly be any value to my voice. So many people were out on social media, blogging, and YouTubing that had big, amazing ideas that I didn't think I could compete with. I felt like anything that I would say would just be a repeat of something someone else had already said. I wasn't unique. Nothing I thought or said was special. Therefore, I read blogs and scoured social media for educational musings, but hesitated every time I considered putting my own thoughts out into the world.

There is a time long ago that I consider my "educational transformation" era. I began to present at conferences. First, because people asked me to, then because I realized that even though I thought my ideas were obvious, there were always people that resonated with them. Of course, there were people who had already heard them as well, but by that time I understood that we were all on our own journeys of learning. There may be someone who knows more than me and those who would like to learn from my experience. Presenting led to blogging and my entire reason for reflecting in a blog post shifted when I realized that while I wrote a blog for others to learn, I needed to focus on blogging for my own professional growth and change. Also, it was my responsibility to give back to the professional learning community that had freely shared ideas with me while I was still developing.

Knowing that others might still wonder about their own voice, I try to invite others to share by modeling vulnerability and openness in my interactions and writing. I am as likely to admit when I make a mistake as when I do something amazing because modeling how to move forward from failure and develop resilience is one way to help others become more open about their own experiences. Sending your voice out into the world can be scary, but understanding that sharing your thoughts both improves your own thinking and gives back to the professional learning community. Putting your fear aside and moving forward is worth it.

• Mandy Froehlich, Speaker, Consultant, and Author of *The Fire Within* and *Divergent EDU*, Appleton, Wisconsin
• Follow on Twitter @froehlichm

BET 12: WHAT'S YOUR WAGER?

The Pit Boss Perspective

*E*very school system has its own culture. The culture of a school or a district can be enhanced or devalued by those who are a part of the system. The actions that you take and the mission that you choose to pursue lets others know what your culture is all about. Consider what your district is focused on right now. Think about the important work happening around you. Reflect on what that work is saying to others. Is your district or school fostering a culture of yes? I didn't realize it, but I had entered into a world of No.

No, you can't buy that.

No, things don't really work like that here.

No, you can't go there.

No, we don't have time for that.

No, we don't do that kind of professional development.

There were so many "Nos" that I wasn't even sure how to get to Yes. Barriers were up everywhere I turned--and I was in central office! I could only imagine how the teachers felt. They had been told no so many times that they simply stopped asking.

I thought, how in the world was I going to overcome this? I had to wager a few bets if I was going to enact change. So, I started taking steps to develop a culture of yes. I looked for small wins with teachers that could build a momentum of yes in our district.

I'd like to paint my room blue. Yes!

Can you help me write a grant to get more technology? Yes!

I was wondering if I could go visit another school that is focused on teaching writing. Yes!

Can a group of us go to the fall Maker Faire? Yes!

Do you think we could finally move that old TV out of my room? Yes!

Is it possible to get more stools for my classroom? Yes!

Teachers started to realize that if they had an idea, it was OK to ask. While I couldn't always say yes, I tried my hardest to provide support to the teachers who were taking a risk and trying to improve learning for our students. We needed to start somewhere.

Jacie continued to ask what we would like to see happen, but for many, trust was not built yet to be able to answer her honestly. In reality, for some, it was never going to be. We each have a story. I think about the professional compliance that steered my teaching methods for years, and I sit in awe. And not the good awe.

As a professional, the expectation was that you responded with compliance as you were the subordinate. It was that simple. There was no room for opinion, risk-taking, or failure that would lead to growth. There was no room for change unless passed *down to you*. This was what we knew. This was how we taught our students. We had teams of educators discussing policy, curriculum, behavior management, and more, but the discussion was not actionable. Why speak up now when before we were always left walking away wondering why we said anything at all?

"May I" was met with responses such as...

Will the entire team be doing it that way?

We will have to discuss it at another time.

There are not enough funds.

There is not enough time.

If I allow you, I will have to allow everyone else too, and I can't.

Not this year.

We do not have the storage to remove that from your room, you will have to keep it.

It is not done that way.

Let me get back to you.

Unlike me, many teachers were not ready to bet on Jacie at this point. For me, I was ready to place a wager... I was ALL IN!

 JACKPOT!

A culture of NO can be debilitating, but a culture of YES can bring about a renewed sense of joy to your school.

DOUBLE DOWN

- Within your role, what steps can you take to create a culture of YES?
- Is there something that you can remove to make room for betterment?

ANTE UP with Julia Bennett Grise

The world of education is more than teaching and learning. It is a complex web of relationships that take time, effort, and genuine passion to build, strengthen, and last. Administrators who create a culture of trust where faculty, staff, and students feel comfortable taking risks or asking for guidance are leaders who truly understand the importance of relationships across the entire district. Furthermore, administrators who provide educators with the opportunity to work with those outside of their district create an even more defined and valuable culture. I, personally, work within a district where the "culture of yes" exists. I have had the opportunity to work alongside teachers from multiple school districts. We have collaborated to (1) strengthen our existing teaching practices to better influence student growth, (2) transform our traditional classes into flexible spaces, and (3) design and create outdoor classrooms that benefit teachers and students while promoting the 4 Cs. This opportunity, which also partners with our local career and technology center, would have never been possible without the support from the administration. A "culture of yes" requires an "all-hands-on-deck" approach, and I am lucky enough to be a part of a work environment that understands the importance of relationship building, collaboration, and a positive culture of support, not just across one district, but the entire county.

• Dr. Julia Bennett Grise, High School Teacher in Beaver, Pennsylvania

ANTE UP with Knikole Taylor

Working with adult learners is a rewarding challenge that I enjoy. Over the past few years, I have learned which wagers to make and which ones to walk away from. At the end of the day, I want teachers to feel respected, honored, and heard. If I am unable to give this to teachers through the task or goal, the cost is too high, and I have no issues walking away.

Allowing teachers to have voice and choice in "how" we accomplish tasks has helped me to create a culture of yes within the various educational communities in which I serve. In education, we often don't have a lot of say in the "what" that we have to do, but I try to ask teachers to help me craft solutions, routines, and procedures. Giving them the space and the opportunity to share their expertise on issues that affect them helps me to honor their voices and knowledge as professionals. While open dialogue in meetings are a welcoming gesture, I have also learned to utilize tools that give teachers the opportunity to speak, especially those teachers who are reluctant to speak out in large groups. Digital tools like Google Docs to flip or blend meetings allow users to type their comments and suggestions to questions posed for an entire learning group or campus. Also utilizing spaces like Facebook and Twitter gives educators the opportunity to respond and be heard. Win!

- Knikole Taylor, K-12 educator
- Follow on Twitter @knikole

BET 13: GO SEE A SHOW

The Pit Boss Perspective

*S*ometimes the players sit at a table so long, they don't even know if it's day or night. They've been playing so intently, so focused on their game that they forget to take a minute and see all that Vegas has to offer. Head to dinner. Go see a show. Get out of the casino and see what else is out there.

We need to do this in education, too. Take an opportunity to get out of the classroom and see what else is going on. Sometimes that might mean taking a walk down the hall to another classroom or visiting another school altogether. There are opportunities all around us if we take the time to notice them.

The opportunity to find out what the hype was revolving around PBL (in this case, Project-Based Learning) was in front of me, and I needed to grab ahold. Some said, if was the wheel wasn't broken, why fix it?

I heard others say...

Isn't this just another way to say thematic unit?

If that's the case, I have this!

Better yet, I did this already.

Nothing new at all!

Ummmm, NO! Not the same... this is NEW! I scrolled through my emails to ensure I was signed up for the workshop. Nothing. I reached out to the district, Avonworth ASD, hosting this new innovative practice, and I was graciously received. Breathing again, I felt this was just what I needed to broaden my plan for the fall.

PBL Works describes Project Based Learning as,

> Students work on a project over an extended period – from a week up to a semester – that engages them in solving a real-world problem or answering a complex question. They demonstrate their knowledge and skills by developing a public product or presentation for a real audience.
>
> As a result, students develop deep content knowledge as well as critical thinking, creativity, and communication skills in the context of doing

an authentic, meaningful project. Project-Based Learning unleashes contagious, creative energy among students and teachers. (PBL Works, n.d.)

PBL... this style of teaching/learning is the epitome of empowerment. I left the three-day workshop feeling like I could do anything. Nothing was in my way, but me! I had to learn more. I had to understand how to connect with my current students. I had to reimagine a better me. I had to find professional development that would take me where I wanted to go!

The possibilities are endless! I am a BELIEVER in possibilities... the kind that can build on passions and personalize learning for each child! As educators, we can switch up the scenario. We can level up the learning for all students. It can happen with a simple shift. Why isolate reading to an anthology? Consider mixing together your resources. Blend together science, social studies, and math with reading skills through Project-Based Learning (PBL) PBL shines the light on:

- Voice and Choice
- Personal Passions
- Empowerment and Engagement
- Student Growth

Yes, these aspects are all different, and some feel that content is "easier" to teach isolated, but how do we continue to teach billions of children the same way when they are each their own unique self, driven by their differences? Think about music and the different genres that allow individuality to surface. Did you ever start dancing, and before you knew it, you were stepping on toes? Or maybe yours were being stepped on. Not because you meant to, but because the music *moved* you in that direction. Just watch a room full of kids dance... are they really dancing to the same song? One is rapping, one is flailing about, another looks like they are doing a new twist to the tango, while someone else is flying solo... sitting in a corner just moving his head up and down. But wait... isn't this what it's all about? So why is everyone shooting the look of... **um, are we dancing to the same music? Maybe the question should be, do we have to be?**

The Pit Boss Perspective

If we worried about stepping on toes, where would we be right now? As educators, we do need to be mindful of the toes we may be stepping on, but ultimately if your toes are in the way of our progress, then you better get off the dance floor!

When you are leading positive change, there will be people who don't hear the music you are hearing. They won't get up and dance, no matter how loud you turn it up. They will look at you funny when you are dancing your heart out, but they'll never join you. That's ok with me.

As administrators, we focus our time and energy on the mission and vision of the district. If we want to move initiatives forward, we need to fuel the teachers who are ready to dance. We need to give them the tools and the opportunities to make it happen.

Here's the truth. If you are a teacher in my district and you want to do better for kids, then I will help you to get connected and do every-

thing in my power to help you do that. I will support you. I will find the funding. I will buy books. I will lift you up in every way to help you succeed. *If you aren't committed to doing what's right for kids and you aren't committed to learning and growing with me, then I will spend my time with those who do. Either you are dancing at this party, or you're not. You decide.*

"There are *opportunities* all around us if

we *take the time* **to** *notice* **them."**

#ALLinEDU

JACKPOT!

Get out of the casino and go see a show. See what else is going on! Take some time out of your classroom, building, or district to learn and grow from those in your learning network.

DOUBLE DOWN

- What will you do this week to get out of the casino and see what eduVegas has to offer?
- Create a plan to head to a local conference or aim

bigger and travel to meet up with your PLN (Professional Learning Network).

- Is there an Edcamp being held nearby?
- Is there a local district or a regional educational service agency such as an Intermediate Unit that is offering a course that could create a new spark in your classroom?
- Maybe YOU can start a #coffeeEDU (a one-hour unconference for educators) in your area, where you inspire other educators to join in and reflect on their practice, discuss a book, or simply be there for one another in support. For more information, go to their website: https://coffeeedu.org/

ANTE UP with Rich Czyz

As an administrator, I have had the opportunity to serve in a couple of very different roles. When I worked as a Supervisor and Director on the Curriculum and Instruction side of a school district, it was easy for me to attend a number of conferences and learning opportunities outside of the district. My schedule allowed flexibility, and I had opportunities to visit other districts to learn about what they were doing to lead and innovate. One of my favorite activities in growing as a learner was visiting other schools in different districts to see how they implemented a certain program or initiative. These visits gave me the opportunity to see firsthand how teachers approached a curriculum program — what the limitations were that would need to be overcome by teachers, and ultimately, what strategies led to success. I was able to ask questions and walk away with classroom-tested answers that helped me in my position.

On the other hand, being a school-based leader (in my current role as principal) doesn't afford the flexibility to attend many conferences during the school year or to visit many other districts or classrooms. Therefore, I rely on opportunities on the weekends to continue my learning and growth as an educator. Two such opportunities that happen frequently in my area are Edcamps and CoffeeEDU. Edcamps are conferences in which the agenda is determined by the participants on the day of the event. The informal nature of these events and allowance for everyone in the room to serve as an expert distinguish these events from more formal conferences where only a few serve as the experts. I enjoy Edcamps for this reason, as I get to learn about the latest and greatest innovative strategies from classroom practitioners. At CoffeeEDU events, several educators gather at a nearby coffee shop on a Saturday or Sunday morning for an hour to chat informally. Gathering with other educators from different backgrounds and districts affords me the opportunity to continue my learning, to hear about something that was done differently, to pick someone's brain about something that I'm struggling with, or to share an idea that I have and receive valuable feedback from other passionate educators. These opportunities allow me to learn from others and collaborate with educators outside of my school setting to provide for my growth as a professional.

- Rich Czyz, Principal at Yardville Elementary School in Hamilton, New Jersey
- Follow on Twitter @RACzyz

BET 14: PENNY JACKPOT

$\mathcal{C}$hange had come! This was the in-service day that did change. The one that went from a sweltering hot auditorium (with a lecture on how we need to be better before we even get our fresh start) to an air-conditioned banquet hall with our high school marching band loudly playing the fight song *just for their teachers*. The change that gives you chills and resets your inspirational compass so that it points straight forward. The kind that has your innovative new administrators challenging you to open a Twitter account and connect with other educators in the crusade to remake learning. The kind of administration that TRUSTS you with social media.

The Pit Boss Perspective

It wasn't just about social media, but it had everything to do with shaking things up. After my first year, we had a new superintendent on board. We held a common vision for how to put students at the center, and it needed to be communicated in a big way. We moved our opening day events to a local banquet hall, provided breakfast, and hopefully some inspiration. We aimed to bring positive energy and a focus on a new era. The high school band played the school alma mater (a surprise that none of the teachers expected). We did things differently, setting the tone for a new year that would be founded on connections with one another and with students.

We had to have a little fun too. We ended the first day together with a bang as we did rock, paper, scissors competition with over 200 faculty and administration. (Although I don't know who started this cool culmination, I give credit to Joe Sanfelippo and Tony Sinanis, who shared the idea at the National Principals Conference a few years back.) It left our teachers feeling pumped up and excited to start a new year. It also sent the message that things were changing in our district.

> **"Positive change can feel like hitting the jackpot when there are strong relationships between teachers and leaders."**
>
> #ALLinEDU

My current administration has brought on many changes... positive changes... innovative changes!

We now have permission to choose how we will teach the

Common Core Standards in our own individual classrooms in place of being on the same page, on the same day, just like all other classrooms in the district.

We now have Tech Fest, an annual event where lead learners step up and share their knowledge to help push our district forward. This in itself is an opportunity to not only connect with our peers but for relevance to technology to blossom through in-house collaboration and real-world application of lessons that are already in use within our very own district. Keep in mind that these "lead-learners" are not necessarily experts (I, for one, dabble in many areas, but have so much more room to grow), but they are risk-takers who are willing to share what they know to pay it forward for every child. Through their vulnerability, they, in turn, are inspiring others to try something new too. It may be learning more about Apple apps, Flip-Grid, Sway, Google apps, Coding, or Makerspace. The list goes on and on as each teacher delves further into their own growth.

We now have trust in choosing flexible seating as an option for a learning environment that challenges and encourages all children.

We now have permission to blend our curriculum so that we are no longer teaching the same concepts in three separate subject areas, such as reading, science, and social studies, according to the map. I never could understand why we devalued the power of content connections just to be faithful to a map. I would find myself teaching a lesson in science on inventions in the fall, inventors in social studies in the middle of the winter, and turning around in the spring to read a biography from the anthology about an inventor in history that had a great impact. My students would question these moments too. It was nothing for a child to say, "Didn't we already learn that?" Well, yes, but...

We now have district goals to engage all students every day, all day — to show purpose, passion, and pride in the school and throughout the community. This change is AMAZING!

JACKPOT!

Change can be an amazing moment of hitting the jackpot or a chance to lose it all and go bankrupt. Both can be incredible takeaways for personal growth.

DOUBLE DOWN

- **How can administrators communicate new learning and change without having teachers interpret it as a personal hit on their teaching?**
- **How can teachers be more open to change, even if their current practice is working for them personally?**
- **What is an area you have grown in that you can help others to learn? Never underestimate your impact!**

ANTE UP with Tina Carbone

I LOVE my profession. Can you say that? Honestly, I can't imagine doing anything else in life that has more meaning and fulfillment than being an educator. For as long as I can remember, I knew I wanted to be a teacher. The awakening for me was the realization that I had wanted to dedicate my life to being in special education. The disappointing surprise was my critics...

" You'll never last in that field."
" There's a high burnout for people who choose that career path."

The discouragement didn't phase me; in fact, it motivated me. I knew that people didn't see the potential that I saw in my students—the strengths among the weaknesses, the gifts beyond the impossibilities. I believed in my underdogs and I can tell you that I have witnessed miracles with my students. I knew this path was where I'd find gratification and purpose.

So, it came as an unexpected twist when I found myself facing that "burnout" that I had been warned about all those many years ago. I remember the moment that burnout smacked me in the face—I was working with a student who was exhibiting some challenging behaviors. I recall feeling frustrated because I had spent an enormous amount of energy preparing the lesson. Suddenly, one of my paraprofessionals spilled into the room to give me the report of another student's misbehavior. I remember a disheartening feeling wash over me. "It's time to cash in my chips" was all I could think. Although I denied it to myself on that day, change had come. It was time. I just needed to give myself permission to let go and grow.

I prayed about taking the risk and jumping into a new classroom. It would be more academically-based. Would I like it? How could I leave my current students and their families with whom I had developed such close relationships? (I mean, after all, they needed me!). I bravely accepted the new position and shared the news with my students and families. Their support was such a blessing and reinforced that this change was going to be okay.

Here I sit a year later in this new position. Friends, I've hit the jackpot! My growth has no limits. I've had opportunities to collaborate with my colleagues, as well as to experience and teach new curriculum while watching my littles surpass all expectations. That "burnout" has been replaced with a renewed viewpoint on myself as an educator and that what I do matters. If I wouldn't have rolled the dice, I would have missed out on the chance to grow into something more. Our students deserve for us to take a chance on change!

• Tina Carbone, Elementary Teacher in Hopewell Area School District, Pennsylvania

ANTE UP with Nicole Ozimok

In my experiences, good fortune comes about when one actively tries to make positive change. In terms of positive change and personal growth, I started out with small incremental changes that allowed me to develop my risk-taking skills and take chances to improve my classroom environment.

A few years ago our district was "lucky" to be newly led by a new team of administrators. Within a very short time, many educators began to implement innovative practices throughout the district. Not being a huge risk taker for the fear of failure, I had certain reservations in implementing these changes as opposed to my fellow educators. Watching from across the hall and being inspired by the environment of my colleague's classroom, it was obvious how much her students loved the opportunities that were made available to them. Wanting to give the same opportunities to my students, I decided to take a gamble and implement some of these new innovative ideas. My first attempt at taking the risk was to introduce the concept of flexible seating.

I loved the positive change I witnessed in my classroom from taking this risk. I had hit a small jackpot in an area that I longed to make better for my students and me their needs. This one change led the way for me to open my mind to new ideas that were at the forefront of education and grow as a learner and educator.

By starting with one risk, I have allowed myself the opportunity to share my successes with others. This new and exciting way of thinking and learning in the classroom has helped me teach myself and others that change is necessary and that with change, you help yourself and others grow. To share my experiences with others and know that I may inspire someone to take a chance, I consider that a positive experience for all involved.

• Nicole Ozimok, Elementary Teacher in Hopewell Area School District, Pennsylvania
• Follow on Twitter @ozimokn

BET 15: IT'S A CRAP SHOOT

For teachers, our profession is in constant change. It can be uncomfortable and scary at times. It can even go as far as to create anxiety in some. We need to find a way to help ourselves through it, for the betterment of every child, and without sacrificing relationships with others. Administration changes, and with that comes different philosophies and goals. Positions change. The curriculum *should* change, yet that is the one thing that many teachers hold so close to their hearts, that changing it is like losing a piece of themselves in the process.

Many are not always willing to embrace change or at times, even give another perspective a chance. Possibly it is hinged on pride or the investment of time that went into creating lessons and worksheets that built off of that very curriculum. Maybe they found success with change and feel that it will once again be successful with the next group of students. Team meetings involving discussion on change can lead to disagreement.

Is it the perception of others that creates a barrier for change, or is it the insecurity of possibly not knowing what triggers the overarching fear that most often leads to the disagreement? Shouldn't some push back be welcomed to better analyze the change that we are trying to orchestrate? Being uncomfortable isn't such a bad thing, as a matter of fact, it is then that I find myself breaking through to a better way for my students. Part of it is the process of reflecting on my practice, and the other is having yet another view to help put mine into better focus.

The one area of change that I find is non-negotiable and yet steers so many of our decisions is that of our students. It is a guarantee that we will have different children each year (unless you are looping). This guarantee comes with a package of different personalities, characteristics, home life, ability levels, experiences, and personal stories.

Planning for the unknown is a bit of a "crapshoot" for each of us, but you simply take a risk and adjust. There will be times that you hit the jackpot, and there will be times that you lose, but leaving the game altogether is never in your cards as a teacher… you must be driven to change for the better. This is not easy for teachers, but it is necessary.

The best teachable moment in this situation is the relationship you build with each of your students. They are the mystery behind the brainstorming. They are the driving force that can turn defeat into a win.

Once we know their story and build a relationship with them

around it, the change that has come is worth the investment time and time again. The same goes for your colleagues and your administrators. You are truly never alone in a world of change... you simply need to take the risk and pull the lever down one more time.

The Pit Boss Perspective

Change is the only constant in education. We have chosen to serve in an ever-changing, forging ahead profession. It has to be that way because education is always evolving. Leaders have to change and evolve too.

Change might be hard on teachers— a low-key superintendent with strengths as a manager might be replaced by a highly-engaged super with strength in the curriculum. When that happens, districts change. Priorities change. Where compliance was once revered, creation and collaboration are now the priority. These leadership changes surely impact classroom teachers. It is, therefore, the job of the administrators to communicate the vision for the district and share the expectations. Sometimes those expectations aren't a part of your wheelhouse. Sometimes those changes are out of your comfort zone. That's why relationships are so important.

In my conversations with teachers, a few have been brave enough to say, "I'm not sure how to accomplish that vision of change, but I am willing to try." I appreciate the honesty and my response is always the same. How can I help you?

When I offer to help teachers, I really mean it. I will come into your classroom. I'll co-teach if you want. I'll cover your class so you can go observe in another classroom. Most teachers are hesitant to take me up on it. They think—is she for real? Is she really going to teach my kids? Yes!

Admin may seem like they are far removed from the classroom, but we walked in your shoes once. I taught kindergarten and first graders who had snotty noses and wet pants. I taught struggling learners to read, to add, and subtract. I've survived meetings with challenging parents. I've made it through years with lousy principals and even worse superintendents. I've been there, so I try to never forget what it was like. If it means that I come into your classroom to help you out, I'll do it. I've been there.

 ### JACKPOT!

Effective leaders don't throw their teams into change unsupported. They jump in alongside them and do whatever it takes to bring about positive change. "Leaders" can be across all roles... admin to teacher, teacher to admin, teacher to teacher, teacher to student, student to student, and even student to teacher.

DOUBLE DOWN

- What is one change happening in your school or district?

- How do you feel about it? Why?
- What might you need to feel better equipped to respond to change?

ANTE UP with Mike Lewis

When I think about taking a gamble and working through defeat and setbacks in education, I cannot help but think about the time that I spent working as an "outsider" of the brick and mortar setting. As a former teacher, building principal, and central office administrator, I always saw myself as a strong educational advocate who could find the best in anyone and bring people from diverse backgrounds together for a common cause... our students' best interests. When a small group of individuals began to challenge my commitment and dedication to that very group (our students), I decided to double down and go all in. In doing so, I took a new position outside of a school district but one that I felt would allow me to have a greater impact on the educational programming in my area. I was leaving behind a position, a district, and a student body that I called my own for more than a decade. I was doing so because I didn't want to be in a place that may ultimately defeat me. Not that it had, but it seemed as though the writing was on the wall. I had never found myself in that position before and being in uncharted waters, I decided to walk away... defeated nonetheless. I found myself at a crossroads yet again. This time, trying to decide whether it is time to gamble.

By chance, a new job opportunity came forward, and it was one that gave me a renewed sense of purpose. Although these last three years away from directly working in a school district have been rewarding, they haven't allowed me to meet my internal needs of why I entered education in the first place. I am a teacher's biggest supporter, an advocate for all students, and a compassionate parent who knows what it is like to see your own child struggle and simply want the best for them. It is all of that and so much more that has again propelled me forward with new energy, new life, and a renewed sense of confidence in knowing that my "all-in bet" is just what I need.

- Mike Lewis, Director of Student Services in Pittsburgh, Pennsylvania
- Follow on Twitter @mlewis_qvsd

BET 16: THE HOUSE ALWAYS WINS—THE EGO IN EDUCATION

*W*ho is this really about . . . this thing we call teaching? Is this about you and your strengths or those of your students? Maybe it's a balance between both. Too often, the pendulum swings way too far towards the teacher. I don't believe that was the foundation that our methods classes were trying to build, but with a few questions, prompts, and even assignments at the collegiate level, I feel we have taken education and made it a teacher-driven profession in place of the student. Think about it... do you remember being asked what your dream classroom would look like? You may have even been given the assignment to draw, label, and present it as I did. What did this assignment do for me as a young, ambitious future teacher? It told me that my classroom was **my dream**, and I could make it anything that I wanted and that it could be successful without ever even meeting my students once, let alone year after year. I mean, come on; do you have any idea how many trips it takes (**to the countless**

stores I peruse each summer) to create the masterpiece dream room I want each year? I... I... I... me... me... me... it is moments like this that I fear the ego is born, if not fueled.

Does it matter if some students need a desk while others are needing to stand up and move around? Not if that wasn't part of my dream, **right?** Was that the intent of that assignment? Surely not, but I know that I walked away dreaming about what I wanted to create. Did you? I see it in my field students, my student teachers, and even my virtual students to some degree. Is this type of assignment telling future educators that they are the ones in full control of the environment that their children will learn in? Not to mention that many of these same future-teachers (is that an oxymoron... future and teacher?) chose this profession based off of their own experience of behavior charts, compliancy, rows of desks, and a teacher at the head of the class with a smartboard upgrade over a blackboard. **Sigh!**

Teachers are full of heart, and they share it readily with their students. One way that they do this is by decorating their classrooms. For some teachers, they are trying to recreate a special environment that will encourage their students. Others are looking to take away the "institutional" feel that comes from the typical white wall, no color classroom. There are so many things to consider when creating this special place for children. What if the teacher loves a lot of decorations, colors, and "stuff" throughout the classroom, yet the child with attention issues cannot find their way to focus past the dream classroom that was built with the utmost love and care? Who is it about now? With the best of intentions, I have been that teacher. When distraction occurred for some students, I was unsure if that was the child or possibly my overstimulation of decor. It left me reflecting and rethinking my dream versus their needs. As a teacher, you may take it personally because you spent your own money creating this dream classroom that is now not being "appreciated" by this student. For me, I even felt that way when items were donated. How could that child pick apart the new cushion chair when I have a basket of fidgets right there to use? Do I put items away until I have a class that can "handle it?" These thoughts have crossed my mind. They steered decisions that I have made. In the end, I had to remember that this was their learning space, and for each child to be successful, I had to find a way to create the best options for them. This became a powerful shift of ownership in my classroom. It started with one on-one-conversations:

How do you learn best? Standing? Sitting? Laying down? With music or without?

Do you need my help choosing a seat in this flexible learning environment? How can I help pick the best seating for you?

What do you need from me, to shine like the star you are?

What about that lesson you created so perfectly that was a smash hit the first year but fell on its face the second with only a few students mastering the concept? Who was it about then? Did you stop and adjust for the students, or did you keep your lesson because you had already found it was successful once before? Who was it about then? Or what about the classroom behavior management project that you had to devise for your methods class without ever meeting the students you were going to teach? I'm not saying that the undergraduate assignments themselves do not have worth; I am simply saying that they nurture a dream in each of us that needs to be open to change!

The only resource you have at the time is yourself, so that is how you devise your plan. There is no way around it, but what happens is it becomes yours... the teachers. A resource you hold on to for the precious value it has... never once seeing the light of day, let alone a classroom, but it is yours, and you cannot wait to use this dream plan in your dream classroom. BUST!

The Pit Boss Perspective

You know you've seen this before. The teacher who wants to teach a special unit every year, because they love it or because they spent a lot of their time designing this unit (possibly 10 or 20 years ago). There are cute activities to connect to the stories that they like. They even have a video to show (hopefully not a VHS tape). It's just the way they have always done things.

Don't get me started on whether this is tied to any relevant standards or if it has any place within the curriculum. Has the teacher stopped to figure out if the students are even interested in this topic? I understand that we've gone to school, received the training, and are the professional educators. We have the skills and resources to make these decisions. For some, turning the decision over to seven/eight-year-olds may sound ridiculous, but reflective educators don't allow their ego to get in the way. They plan with students in mind. They give students ownership over their learning. Reflective educators respond to the changing needs and interests of the students they serve. They recognize that last year's lesson plans can't be duplicated for this year's students.

Why do we continue to do things over and over without pausing to reflect on our practices?

It's not about you.

It's about the kids.

Let's try something new! Or not! I have heard some teachers say they simply would not try something new or different because they did not like it, or they did not find worth in it. Did they ask their students? Have you ever heard a student ask a question that the teacher did not have the answer to? Think about what the teacher did. Did they shut the question down, or did they embrace it and allow their own vulnerability of not knowing lead to new learning?

I remember one student with a variety of life experiences. Some of them became his areas of expertise, while others were little sparks that simply needed fuel added to them to really light them up. Along his journey of learning, he struck up a conversation with his teacher about one of his passions. Who would have ever thought that this exact encounter would be life-changing, and not for the better? His teacher shut him down. Not just the conversation, but his excitement for learning. The teacher told that student he knew a lot about nothing. On that very day, that child stopped learning. He stopped believing in himself and education. That child, that student, my son.

Was this my mistake? Did I set my sons up for failure? I was the mom who left my basement unfinished for making, creating, tinkering, and messiness. I encouraged my sons to take things apart to see how they were made... what made them tick. I never said no to a book no matter what day or what store we were in. This was key to their curious minds. If they saw a lizard on the front of a book, they grabbed it. A landscape of the mountains, they grabbed that too! A map fell into the shopping cart. A guide for reptiles, toss it in! I didn't just build a relationship for my sons with learning; I let their passions unfold and then got out of the way. This was an adventurous way to grow up... an exhilarating start to lifelong learning, but the reality was that I set them up for failure.

I helped them realize that their interests mattered. That they, too, had a voice in their learning. Some of their teachers were passionate about writing, so they wrote. Some were passionate about science, so they experimented. It came down to their teacher's passions, interests, and expertise. What about students' passions? What about their interests? This didn't just become an academic issue for my eldest; this became a behavior problem. A reaction to his resentment. The rebelling had begun.

By the time he had encountered teachers that were willing to hear his voice, he was too full of resentment to share. This became a reflection on him somehow and not the system that he was at the mercy of with his learning. Don't get me wrong., he himself will tell you that he owns many of his poor choices, but for me as his mom and as an educator, I can't help but wonder if that couldn't have unfolded differently.

The toughest of times can offer some of the biggest rewards. Through love and determination on the part of our family, and the open hearts of several educators, including many administrators, my son was able to find the sweet spot in learning. Although there were many hurdles that he continued to face, he was blessed with empathy and understanding, along with a growth mindset to foster student voice. In the big picture, he was able to find "his people" amongst his teachers. The ones who recognized his gifts, his ability, his passions, his fears, his heart. Those teachers have created an impact that will forever pay forward for our son.

 **JACKPOT!**

When we hold tight to the things that are important to us, sometimes we let our egos get in the way. If we keep our focus on the kids, we will surprise ourselves at our willingness to open our mindset and embrace new ideas!

DOUBLE DOWN

- **Write down one thing that you are still holding on to that may be more for your comfort zone than that of your students.**
- **Can you meet the change halfway and embed a new strategy within the lesson idea that you covet?**

ANTE UP with Donna Steff

As the teacher, and the authority in the classroom, you don't have to always be right. When I started teaching, I was taught by my mentor and other experienced teachers around me to have a solid set of rules for my classroom. It would make classroom management easier they said. I was instructed to make those rules air-tight, so that if a student, or worse yet a parent, questioned what I was doing, there was always a solid response in the syllabus handed out on day one. But as my years of teaching progressed, so did my mindset. I started to wonder. What if things were more fluid? What if I gave students the opportunity to explain themselves before delivering a canned answer? What if I allowed the student (gasp!) to be right?

Students often question the reason for doing things in class: Why do we have to do this? Can I turn this in tomorrow? Is this for a grade? And the answer is usually "because those are the parameters set by the syllabus" or "because I said so". Often these conversations were followed by a parent phone call or email asking for more clarification. If I had listened to my advisors, my answer would have been, "that's the way it is, those are the rules, and there's nothing I can do about it."

But why does it have to be that way? What if we asked students to come up with a solution WITH us instead of the teacher always handing out the rules. It isn't easy, but it builds better relationships within the classroom and gives students the opportunity to take ownership of their behavior and school work. I've found that this approach also changes the parent phone call conversation to something like this, "Thanks so much for helping Suzie figure out what to do since she missed turning in that assignment on time. We all really appreciate your help."

I have built so many positive relationships with students and parents because I have conversations WITH them instead of AT them. Everyone wants to be successful. Some students just have not figured out how to make that happen. They are still in the trial and error phase of life, often making more errors and not knowing how to help themselves overcome them. I truly believe our jobs as teachers go beyond content. When we teach kids how to be gracious and kind, supportive and reflective, we give them the tools they need to go out into the world ready for success.

• Donna Steff, Junior High English Teacher in Hopewell, Pennsylvania
• Follow on Twitter @DonnaSteff

BET 17: I'LL RAISE YOU

*N*o excuses. There are game-changing opportunities in the paths of educators impacting the lives of so many children. The question is, are they willing to take it? If not, what is it that is holding them back? Is it insecurity formulated within themselves? Is it an insecurity that has been created through past judgment? Is it pride? The feeling of not knowing how to pursue something or to hurdle an obstacle because it may mean that you will be forced to acknowledge an area that you lack? Part of creating change is owning the moment— to take the opportunity presented and raise it to a new level.

You never heard of **that new concept? I'll Raise You... Find out about it!**

You aren't sure how to have your students create a digital footprint or at the very least, share a Google Doc with you? **I'll Raise You... Ask someone!**

Your students would like to learn something that they are passionate about, but you cannot find a way to connect it to the standards you are responsible for teaching? **I'll Raise You... Ask your students to problem solve this with you!**

You are the teacher. You are the professional

The one who creates an opportunity for students to connect beyond the walls of your classroom!

The one who links their passions to their learning.

The one who makes building a relationship with every student a priority.

And this, in itself, is the key to all learning. When we, as educators, are open to new ideas and can model problem solving through vulnerability and inquiry, we are showing our students that we, too, are open to change. We are saying that their questioning and their moments of wonder are an exciting direction for their learning, not a "call out" on what we don't know. That moment when a child is wondering can go either way. It can be a door wide open or one that gets slammed in their face. We must realize that by living in a world that is one click away from more, that it would be ludicrous for educators to feel they must have the answer to every question or that it is a cast of judgment when we don't.

I'll Raise You... to open your mind to learning alongside your students. Gift them the chance to take a moment a step further.

I'll Raise You... the ability to believe that every child can bring something new to learning.

The Pit Boss Perspective

As administrators, we have to push, listen, encourage, give, direct, and organize, but we also have to believe. We have to believe in the faculty that we have hired to do this all-important work. We need to trust that our teachers are making decisions in the best interest of our students. We have to believe in our students and their ability to achieve and persevere. Often times, we have to believe in those around us when they have lost the will to believe in themselves.

We wear a lot of hats as building principals and district administrators. Just like our team of teachers, we have a lot on our plates, and it can be challenging to juggle all of our responsibilities. It can be easy to get tunnel vision and focus on a few key initiatives. When we are focused on driving new programs and working on system-wide change, we cannot lose sight of those who are right in front of us.

Reflect on the players in your EDUcasino. How can you meet them where they are but also say, "I'll raise you?" Do you know where your teachers are in their professional development or in the development of their instructional practices? Get out into the classrooms and have these much-needed conversations. Listen to their areas of strengths and needs. That's right, listen. Stop telling them to do this or implement that. Find where they are currently and support them as they are looking to grow. Create opportunities for those who are ready to take a gamble. Be the constant resource for teachers who are ready to ante up!

 **JACKPOT!**

We have game-changing opportunities every day. Know that in this connected world, we cannot feel like we have all the answers. You can only raise yourself up if you know you have somewhere better to go.

DOUBLE DOWN

- Identify an area of personal insecurity and think about how you can raise the jackpot.
- Pick one person who has that as an area of strength and create a connection with them.

ANTE UP with Rachelle Dene Poth

Over the last couple of years, I came to realize that while I thought I was doing a lot of different, fun, and engaging things for my students, the reality was, I had it all wrong. I completely misunderstood what student engagement looked like. My teaching practice was repetitive, and I was using the wrong lens to view student success. I was teaching the same way that I had been taught.

As a student who was successful in learning languages, I thought that what worked for me would work for my own students. The methods, activities, homework assignments, projects, the structure of the class lessons, you name it, were patterned after what I experienced and what I thought exemplified the look and feel of a successful classroom.

A year of struggling to engage students and not under-standing why they weren't learning and why I wasn't reaching them forced me to take a close look at myself. How had I been preparing for my students and my classroom every day? By repeating the same process. A big piece that was missing was I was not asking my students for feedback. What didn't they understand and what was or was not working for them? I was settled in my methods and using only those which *I* was comfort-able with.

When we "up our game," it means we are willing to bet on ourselves. We push back against the odds that some-thing may or may not work. We try our luck, hoping for the best and trying to improve in some way. For me, it means that I put myself out there more and make connections, not only with members of my PLN but more importantly, by staying connected to and working with my students.

I am intentional about learning something new each day and of not being afraid to take risks with what may seem to be crazy ideas that won't ever work. When we know better, we do better, and now I know that I have to take those chances. To stay on top of my game, I must place bets knowing that I might lose big but recognizing that innovation and learning does not happen without taking risks. We stay on top when we lean in and listen to students for ideas and connect and learn together. We show our students that no matter what happens, we are willing to take chances because win or lose, the payoff no matter how big or small is that we are learning and growing together. There is always something to improve upon. Take the time to connect, reflect, and never settle for the status quo. Our work is too important.

• Rachelle Dene Poth, Educator and Consultant in Pittsburgh, Pennsylvania,
• Follow on Twitter @Rdene915

ANTE UP with Chris Woods

Educators, I know you're super busy. I'm busy too. Our responsibilities include teaching, assessment, all kinds of paperwork, and reports. Not to mention family duties at home. Maybe even volunteer work or a second job. So when we "raise the pot" or go "all in," we do it because we really believe in the hand we've been dealt. We want to win. And "winning" means being better for the kids in our classrooms and schools. But I'm guessing your first thought on getting better is going to conferences. But I don't wait around to attend a conference to get better; I try to get better every day. How?

By reading great books.

By listening to podcasts.

By spending time on Twitter.

There are so many great books out there. Educators are stepping up and sharing their experiences in the classroom, their tips for a better classroom, their ideas for how they'd like to see education change. If you don't know what books to try, ask a colleague in your school what books they've read lately. Podcasts are perfect for becoming a better educator. I love listening to educational podcasts while driving to and from school, while working on a project in the yard, or while going for a walk. And many of these include interviews with real teachers sharing their best ideas. It's like attending a conference session without having to make sub plans. Yes, there's plenty of politics on Twitter, but it's also filled with educators. I like to spend three minutes while waiting in line or 15 minutes while eating my lunch scrolling through the links to blog posts, inspirational quotes, and pictures and videos straight from classrooms all across the world. So many of these can be used in my classroom tomorrow or spark an idea of something I can do to engage my kids. Oh, and if you've never participated in a Twitter chat, you really need to try. There are chats based on every subject, grade level, and specialty. It's like a teacher lounge discussion with a bunch of educators just like you. Try something. Don't wait to get better. Raise the pot and go all in!

• Chris Woods, High School Teacher
• Follow on Twitter @dailystem

BET 18: THE EYE IN THE SKY

The Pit Boss Perspective

*T*here are plenty of people in your life who will try to pull you down. Sometimes they are friends or family members. Sometimes they are neighbors or co-workers. In school, this is no different. There will always be those people who don't like that you are trying something new. They won't like that you are going outside of the textbook (gasp!). They won't like that you are having a conversation with an administrator. My response to those people--get over it!

I am not the eye in the sky, sitting in my office watching the cameras and looking for people to screw up. I choose to spend my time out in our schools, keeping a pulse on the progress of our district. I choose to walk the halls, check out student work, and talk with our staff and students.

Yes, I am an administrator, and some traditional admin don't believe that they can befriend teachers. I will tell you this--I have benefitted in my educational career by surrounding myself with amazing people who make me laugh, push my thinking, and live for the learning. They challenge me to consider new ideas and ask the hard questions. They wonder and argue and brainstorm and try. They do this every day because they want to make schools better for kids.

I don't care if you work in the cafeteria, or are a custodian, secretary, paraprofessional, or teacher — if you are going to help me to be a better educator, then I will take the time to get to know you and be your friend.

Some call them naysayers, but I call them fun-suckers! A naysayer can be described as a person who criticizes or opposes something. I have found myself at the end of a naysayer more than once, and most often, it is in retaliation to the fun, growth, and overall change that I am trying to create with learning. Change isn't isolated to the learning that I am trying to ignite within my classroom for my students, but also for my colleagues, PLN, and myself.

My relationship with Jacie is no exception. It in itself has also been under fire at times. Some question how I can support so many ideas that create angst and discomfort for them as teachers. Others often allude to the idea that I don't see a teacher's perspective clearly because I associate and build friendships with administrators. For me, it is not about a title, it is all about people! I lean into goodness... the kind that opens the door for my learning and in turn, my students. The kind that stays focused on the children. My relationships are built with people of all titles from around the globe. My friendships and working relationships have grown with custodial staff, cafeteria staff, secretaries, counselors, the tech department, and more. We are all in this together, and by supporting one another and appreciating different perspectives, we are able to lead a revolution on change for our students.

I am a lot like a chameleon when it comes to friendships, learning, and growing. I can jump into new and different conversations and blend right in because I am trying to see it from a new perspective. I can have conversations around debatable topics because I can change my view by looking through a different lens. Being a chameleon has helped me to grow in many ways because I have found a way to change my ideas and my views based on the different conversations. Jacie and I spend time finding ways to open doors, to gain momentum where small sparks are lit. We brainstorm the next step before the current one is behind us. We collaborate on topics of interest. We find ways to shine the spotlight on students' strengths and mastermind plans to strengthen their weaknesses. We jump in on random opportunities that fall in our lap at the last minute. We change the game and embrace new rules along the way.

Then there are the other days. The days on which we talk about family. We talk about our kids, swim lessons, baseball games, and whatever else lands on the calendar that week.

The Pit Boss Perspective

I find it a little crazy that people outside of a relationship take so much time speculating about what's happening on the inside. Are they really worried about the things we talk about? Well, here's the inside scoop. Our relationship is like most relationships. We have our ups and downs. We laugh, mostly about ridiculous things, about adult things, about life things. We argue, mostly about school things. These come from a source of passion that turns into heated discussions. Like most relationships, we have social time and quiet time (and lots of writing time). Our relationship is one of "give-and-take" in which we have found a friend to push us to be better in all aspects of our lives, not just our school lives. Our relationship extends far beyond our professional role as a teacher and an administrator. It's about our relationship as people.

How did that happen? How did we break the stigma of mixing outside our EDUSocialCircle? It simply wasn't about us... kids first, always! From there, the rest unfolded!

JACKPOT!

You will hit the ultimate jackpot when you realize that ignoring titles and focusing on kids is what really matters. Develop relationships with positive people who want to improve teaching and learning. Remember, you do have options that prove to be of great impact beyond your own four walls.

DOUBLE DOWN

- Who can you reach out to to widen your EDUSocialCircle?
- Who can you lean on for support?
- Who may be the one to give you push back to help you grow?
- Who might be the one to broaden your view on life and diversity?
- Who can you ask to help get you connected?
- Take a step to have a conversation with someone outside of your existing circle.

ANTE UP with Kyle Hamstra

I love serving as an educator. To me, there's no journey more sacred than interacting with others to learn, *together*. The very fabric in which we grow as people and professionals is intricately interwoven, one relationship at a time. It's intersections like these in which my perspectives are enhanced.

A lifelong learner at heart, I think critically about how I can improve my craft. We no longer live in times in which we are confined to our four walls, or even one classroom, campus, district, or state. In fact, our potential to become better may be directly correlated to the personal connections (near and far) that we endeavor to sustain.

One educator who modeled the way for making professional learning connections in my life was Dr. Steven
Weber (@curriculumblog). I once heard that he started
the Edcamp movement in North Carolina and he
invited me to my very first Edcamp to learn with others.
At many Edcamps to follow, I observed Dr. Weber literally and figuratively stand alongside others, showing
them how to utilize tools such as Twitter and Voxer to
build a professional learning network. Now, I strive to do
the same, modeling and sharing connections with
others.

Dr. Weber has authored hundreds of blogs, a timeless
archive I frequent to learn about topics such as curriculum, leadership, learning environments, and administration. One of the first bloggers I knew, I consulted him
with a draft of my own first blog, and I like how he
provided feedback in a way that was helpful to me. His
daily tweets provoke me to reflect, thinking about how I
can apply his research and best practices to my daily
walk.

Not only does he lead by simple invitation, profound
dialogue, and a witty sense of humor, Dr. Weber's
mission is to grow the very people he influences. Simply
put, he's not in it to gain followers; he serves to multiply
leaders. I've personally experienced this. He makes me
feel like I'm leading *with* him--not just learning *from*
him. As a result, he's inspired me to pursue leadership
with a vision that's "we-opic" instead of "me-opic". Not
only has Steven proven this collaborative, mountain-

climbing journey to be true, but it's also this authentic and effective leadership style that still shines in our interactions today.

I'm super grateful that long distance, state lines, and the test of time were no obstacles for our relationship. Having confided in Steven with specific questions about career, conferences, and interpersonal matters over the years, I'm realizing his emphasis on my journey all over again. He has changed my practice and approach to education. Dr. Weber provided me with many leadership opportunities, networking strategies, and resources to become better. One of the leaders who first shared Voxer with me, it's amazing to know that he's *still* just a Vox away. I'm thankful for his mentoring over the years. he will always be a lighthouse to guide me as a growing educator, and the eye in the sky to shape my lifelong learning perspectives.

- Kyle Hamstra, STEM Specialist in North Carolina
- Follow on Twitter @KyleHamstra

BET 19: WHAT HAPPENS IN VEGAS . . .

The Pit Boss Perspective

*Y*ou know the phrase--what happens in Vegas, stays in Vegas. It's the idea that the risks you take in Sin City, you should take to the grave. Within the classroom, we need to ban the Vegas rule, because what happens in the classroom should never stay right there... we must connect, network, trust, and build relationships for the betterment of our children!*

Learning can (and should) extend beyond the classroom in any way possible. If it means that we can connect student learning to the world outside of our classrooms, then it is our responsibility to do so. If we can tap into our personal connections to make deeper, more personal learning experiences for our students, then we must. In turn, the great things happening within our classrooms need to be shared beyond the boundaries of our schools. Look for ways to extend your Vegas experience beyond the initial visit.

Over the last few years, I have had the privilege of being a virtual cooperating teacher for future educators of Grove City College in Grove City, Pennsylvania. Education majors are required to take a technology course. One of the professors, and author of <u>EduMagic: A Guide for Pre-Service Teachers</u>, is Dr. Sam Fecich. **She is a true change agent**! She is connecting our future teachers to classrooms while instilling skills for both the future leaders in education as well as the current classroom teacher. Her students are building their PLN (Professional Learning Network) on Twitter and engaging in meaningful learning with a variety of resources, including the book posted above. Pre-service teachers are no longer creating work to be assessed in a silo experience. Better yet, they are connecting with classroom teachers to tie-in their own assignments to K-12 content. In turn, students become their authentic audience, providing rich feedback from personal experience that is invaluable at the collegiate level. Dr. Sam, along with the education department of GCC, is making a change in current practice... investing in our future!

I received an email from Dr. Fecich—an email that I could've easily discarded, but she was asking about a new opportunity that our district had not experienced. I needed to forward it onto someone. Her idea of virtual student teachers was something I hadn't heard of before, but what a smart idea: connecting pre-service teachers early on in their careers with experienced teachers through Skype. I imme-

diately thought of Kristen and forwarded the email. No pressure, but check out this opportunity. She did and loved the experience so much that she shared the idea with her colleagues.

Our district now hosts several virtual students each semester. They provide our classrooms with new tech ideas that connect to grade-level content. Our teachers benefit from fresh ideas. The Grove City students benefit from getting specific and immediate feedback from students and teachers.

If we really want to educate future teachers to be amazing change agents, we need to build relationships at all levels. Colleges, universities, public and private school systems, along with the community and workforce... we must sit down at the same table and break bread together. We need to share in the same meal, prepared by the same hands, and with immense compassion and understanding have the conversation that we share in the responsibility to make a change for the better.

That doesn't end with administrators to administrators more than it is with teacher to teacher. That goes beyond, right into the classroom and out again. Students need the opportunity to share their learning and learn from others. They need to understand that by sharing, they are magnifying their impact tenfold. They are lighting a spark for others and igniting a fire even more.

When we keep our learning in a silo, we also keep our growth in a silo. If we want more, we must give, ask, and create more. All too often, educators hold on to their work in a way that is quite territorial. They made it, and they either want credit for it, or they want others to work just as hard as they did to create their own. Why does this happen? At what point have we shined the spotlight on educators as a singular entity? What teacher do you know who hasn't grabbed an idea off of the front of a magazine, or at a birthday party, or maybe even a website? Teachers have shaped the art of iteration for generations, so why keep our ideas to ourselves? The more we share, the more we get back in return.

I am beyond blessed to work with some of the most incredibly giving educators. Whether it is my third-grade team, Nicole Ozimok and Nicole Parrish, along with our Learning Support teacher Lauren Kozel and Paraprofessional Karen Langton, or reaching out into the hallway to our 4th-grade team Anna Kostrick, Kim Petrina, and Jenny Marchionda, each is an open resource for one another.

"Did you see that post on Twitter?" one pipes in and shares.

"How about a book tasting," says another.

"Let's get together and find a way to really get to know each other's kiddos," one suggests.

And it doesn't stop there... it goes beyond our homerooms and dips into our Technology Instructor, Kait Dailey; Music Teacher, Jenny Kobaly; former PE Teacher, Lisa Morell; Art Teacher, Arlene Nalli; and Librarian, Kathy Bauldoff. To truly create an impact, we rely on the collaboration of this team. If we have something that can create a richer experience for a child, we share out beyond our four walls. We may not have the opportunity to sit down and roadmap an entire PBL together, but if we possess a resource that will enhance the learning process, we share! We must take in other ideas and opinions to grow, and in turn, we must share out to give back on the investment made into each of us. Keep feeding the slot machine of opportunity, and it will spit out tokens in return.

The Pit Boss Perspective

Why are we conditioned to think that learning only happens within the four walls of the classroom? It' may be because that was our personal experience or that is the way that we were taught in our teacher education programs. In some areas, thinking beyond the reach of those walls is unimaginable. They have clearly not felt the power of a global learning network. The relationships that we build as educators can dramatically impact our students, for better or worse.

 JACKPOT!

Learning is limitless! Extend student learning beyond the classroom and welcome others to create an impact.

DOUBLE DOWN

- What is one thing that you recently created that you can share out beyond your own immediate team?
- Break down the walls! What is one way that you can share beyond your own district and community?

ANTE UP with Ciara Cutone

Throughout the year my main focus is the students and their learning experiences. I want them to have control of their learning and what they received from the content that is being taught. On more than a couple of occasions, I have had something planned; however, the students veered onto a different path and we would go the distance. My passion is to find ways to bridge that gap between what my students need and the ways we can connect learning in different ways. Throughout my career, I have tried to use authentic teaching and learning, never afraid to try an out-of-the-box idea.

One of the easiest ways to expand learning is by transforming the classroom to simulate a field trip to a different place. We have had a football classroom transformation to study place value. Every time I do a transformation, I am blown away by how the smallest details can bring so much excitement to my students. Another time, we donned our surgeon attire for the "Prefix and Suffix Surgery Room" where they had to perform surgery on words. Lastly, students put on their police officer badges and went into the hallway where there was a "Contraction Crime Scene" set up, and they had to fill out slips to fix each contraction crime. Every experience was full of excitement, lots of learning, and memories to last a lifetime. By providing my students with these experiences and exposing them to this new learning happens when we make connections. This allows students to be engaged in collaborative conversations that may not have happened had I not allowed the expansion of learning.

• Ciara Cutone, Elementary Teacher in Hopewell Area School District, Pennsylvania
• Follow on Twitter @cutonecr34

ANTE UP with Stan Whiteman

Educational opportunities for students in my district can be summed up in one word: INNOVATIVE. But, unfortunately, this isn't what always comes to mind. This word, "innovative," could not always be said about Duquesne. Nearly 12 years ago, the district was struggling financially and it was difficult to provide a quality education for its high school students. In 2007, Duquesne High School was closed and students were sent on a tuition basis to two neighboring districts. In 2012, Duquesne Middle School followed suit. Back then, these were the only stories that were being told about Duquesne. Now, through the help of social media, our teachers and administrators are telling what really happens at Duquesne.

The district began to reshape its image through its innovative practices and sharing these practices with the digital community via Twitter. Now, nearly half of our staff, including the district office, uses Twitter to document the high-quality learning activities that are

166 | ALL IN!

happening every day. At least one person at each grade level is tweeting regularly. Through Twitter we are able to capture the excitement, engagement, productive struggle and perseverance of our students. Through a short caption and maybe a picture or two, we can show the world the true story of Duquesne City. This is not a school that suffers to provide its students with the best anymore. Our district is paving the way in MakerEd and STEAM learning. In the past four years, we have repurposed four classrooms to create two maker spaces, an updated library media space, and a coding and robotics lab.

It is often said that if you don't tell your own story, someone else will. We are rewriting our script each day and sharing the innovative experiences happening in our school and the world deserves to see.

- Dr. Stan Whiteman III, Director of Curriculum, Instruction, Assessment, and Technology, Duquesne, Pennsylvania
- Follow on Twitter @StanWhiteman

BET 20: DOUBLE DOWN ON YOUR PLN

*Y*ou better sit back and buckle up for this one... it's going to be a ride! There was once a time when I thought that I was alone. Alone in my own thoughts. Alone in my planning. Alone in my teaching. I thought I was isolated from the world and that the only relationships that I was going to have were the ones that were surrounding me in my very own district. Don't get me wrong; I have an amazing crew around me with my own team, my wing, and my go-to people in my district. They give me strength when I am weak, they give me hope when I lack faith, and they push me forward as far as they know to go. But, there is a saying that you are only as strong as your weakest link... I am here to say that was me at times.

So, where do you go from there? I took a challenge, one that Jacie tossed my way in a room full of people that would hold me accountable. She challenged me to join Twitter. Are you kidding me? Not only would I be going against all of the directives that forbid it, but then I would separate myself from my colleagues who were completely against it. How was I going to do this? My gut knew this was the opportunity that I had been looking for... the one that had forward-thinking mindsets just waiting to support me, but my heart was worried about closing in my circle just a little more. I walked to my car. I stopped. I prayed. It was so clear to me at that moment what my purpose was... it was all about the kids, and if that meant getting on social media to make myself a greater value to them, then that was exactly what I was going to do! This very moment was career-changing! It was life-changing for my students, my colleagues, and me!

The Pit Boss Perspective

I joined Twitter in 2014. As a new mom, I was home on maternity leave and missing connections to my school family. I was completely exhausted and certainly didn't have time to read books or stay current with a needy newborn at home. I had recently read Digital Leadership by Eric Sheninger (2014) and was compelled to create an account. This tool would be my new lifeline. As I woke up for 3 am feedings, I would scroll through my Twitter feed. While I didn't have hours to read books, I did have 5-10 minutes to read blog posts. As my little one cried in his crib, I sat in the hallway, waiting for him to fall asleep and hopped on Twitter. Knee-deep in dirty diapers and baby bottles, it was an easy way for me to stay connected to education. It has been, for me, the best personalized professional learning tool imaginable.

So, I was concerned when I found out that the app was blocked in my new school district. It wasn't blocked because there had been any issues. It was blocked because of fear. Fear that social media was evil. Fear that someone would do something wrong. Fear of the unknown.

When I arrived in the district and started encouraging teachers to connect using Twitter, they looked at me like I was crazy. "Don't you know that's not allowed?" I struggled to understand why teachers (and students) were forbidden to use the powerful tools in their hands to connect with others beyond the classroom. I was on a mission to change this from taboo to common practice.

This moment happened because Jacie knew better and then challenged me to be better. She handed me a gift... a jackpot! I was rolling in it... an additional team of educators, new views, solid supports, positive vibes, an abundance of leadership, endless resources, challenging conversations, and so much more!

This was a jackpot alright, but how do you possibly put an amount on a PLN (Professional Learning Network) that has your back 24 hours/day and seven days a week? How do you explain to others that you are better because you are now surrounding yourself with a powerful full house? Never underestimate the power of choice. It all starts with you!

Sharing and learning within my district became a no-brainer for me... "blowing the walls off" of my own room was an easy step in the right direction. But to truly put myself out there, I knew I had to share with the world, literally.

A few ways that this can be done are to:

- Blog and connect it to social platforms to share
- Add a webcam to your class wish list.
- Learn how to use GHO (Google Hangout), Skype, Facetime or some platform of connectivity that is permitted in your district.
- Connect on Social Media and SHARE... give away your best idea and allow it to resonate with others. Take the opportunity to learn from others.
- Join Educational Twitter Chats that build you up and connect you to higher learning, reflection, EDUrelationships, and overall growth.
- Join a Book Study through Voxer. Matt Larson and Ricardo Garcia have ongoing studies that will enrich your world (#2menandabook).
- Join a Voxer Group that is comprised of educators nationwide and from every role within education, such as #4OCFpln. This group emerged from a book study based on Rich Czyz's book, The Four O'clock Faculty: A Rogue Guide for Revolutionary Professional Development. From a single book study to countless studies, emerging friendships, and conversations that grow our own mindset daily, this crew has become family and has truly enriched my life.

If you are interested in any of these opportunities and need more information, reach out through Twitter or email me at nankr1120@gmail.com

JACKPOT!

 Social media can transform your relationships and connect you with a network of educators to provide support and inspiration. As Maya Angelou reminds us, "Do the best you can until you know better. Then when you know better, do better." This is especially true when it comes to social media.

DOUBLE DOWN

Each district and school community has its own culture.

- What inspiration have you found outside of your school district that has helped to move you forward?
- What is one way you can contribute in place of consuming?
- What is something new you can learn and share out with others?

ANTE UP with Wendy Hankins

A wise educator once said, "One tweet was all it took."

An educator, a principal, and author of *The Pepper Effect*,

Sean Gaillard, was referring to the power of social media, specifically Twitter, and says that "just one tweet was an entry point for [his] growth as a connected educator." It all began when Dr. Jennifer Williams, who Sean calls Jen, simply sent out a tweet seeking the advice of other educators. She was just asking for suggestions for fun books to read. That, in turn, led to a collaboration with Sean, which led to the two presenting together at several conferences and, undoubtedly, morphed into a long-lasting friendship.

It was about a year ago when I read Sean's quote, and while I had been "on Twitter" since 2013, I had not used Twitter to my advantage. I would tweet here and there, but I did not really connect with many other educators. Then last spring, in March 2018, I really started seeking out others, reading other educators' blogs, participating in chats, and making real connections. I got ideas. I got inspired. I got connected. On those days where I was struggling, I found myself grabbing my phone to get a dose of positivity, which in turn inspired me to tweet daily messages of positivity and kindness via #HeardIt-FromHankins. After a couple of months, other educators were reaching out to me. I still remember the day Adam Welcome direct message me and asked, "Hey Wendy, do you want to moderate the #KidsDeserveIt chat in July one Wednesday?" Needless to say, I said yes.

Then there was Friday, March 22, 2019. I had connected with *What's Under Your Cape?* author, Barbara Gruener, who had generously offered to come to our #Kindness-

KidsAtKirk Genius Hour class and teach a lesson. The morning she arrived, the front desk called. I excitedly walked to the front office, opened the door, and smiled from ear to ear when I saw Barbara...then shrieked when I saw the author of "Passion For Kindness," Tamara Letter, who was standing next to her. Tamara had flown all the way from Virginia to meet up with Barbara and visit our class. How lucky were our kids to learn about kindness from two of the kindness giants in education?

"One tweet is all it took." It's true. One tweet is all it takes. To express our opinions. To share our voice. To connect with others. To make an impact.

One tweet.
One connection.
One purpose.

The power of connecting with others is impactful, inspiring, and worth indulging in--for it is for one purpose--to grow as educators and be better for kids. So, if you ever--or you hear anyone else--ask, "Why Twitter?" The question should be, "Why not?"

• Wendy Hankins, Educator in Houston, Texas
• Follow on Twitter @MrsHankinsClass

ANTE UP with Jess Hill

Over the past year and a half, I have had the pleasure of being part of a PLN comprised of teachers from various grade levels, disciplines, and districts. In my thirteen years of teaching, most of the networking I had done was within my own middle-level grades and safely inside the comfort zone of my own ELA compadres. Comfort is a dangerous thing: too much of it and you are not taking the risks that you need to grow.

My current partnership with teachers outside of this zone has emboldened me to make noticeable changes in my classroom. With them as cheerleaders and strategic sounding boards, I have incorporated flexible seating options, mindful, meditative reading practices, and more growth mindset-oriented lessons and assessments. The students in my classes have responded to these developments in overwhelmingly positive ways. They look forward to choosing where to sit and work, ask to independently read more often, and have been more open to seeing wrong answers as opportunities for growth.

In addition to the hustle and bustle of learning grammar, analyzing texts, and writing essays, my kids take time to breathe, to choose a better mindset, and to make choices in literature and curriculum that best fit their needs and interests. The culture in my classroom has changed for the better, a shift that makes me grateful for my networking experiences. My PLN and I plan to continue our collaboration, and this gives me the strength to take more chances. Just as my students are getting ideas from and sharing opinions with countless others via social media, so too does my PLN serve as a group from which I gain inspiration for innovation. It is much easier to go out on a limb when others are encouraging you, or better yet, going out there with you.

• Jess Hill, High School Teacher in Beaver, Pennsylvania

BET 21: CHALLENGE THE PIT BOSS

The Pit Boss Perspective

A Vox comes in from Kristen. It's a long one. If you're on Voxer, you know there's an unwritten rule that you are supposed to limit your voxes to 2-3 minutes. When you get one that's close to five minutes, you know you're in trouble. She's fired up, I can immediately tell from her voice. It's about report cards, a change that I initiated. While well-intentioned with this new report card, she's concerned that we aren't giving teachers enough time to complete them with fidelity. Why did we include this? What's the rationale for that? She's pushing, but for a good reason. She knows her students well and doesn't want this new grade reporting tool to take away from the depth of what she wants to share with parents and students. There's got to be a better way, she implores.

Part of the message is that she needs to vent. She needs someone who will hear her out and validate her concerns. Don't we all need that once in a while? A larger part of it is her need to understand. She's not complaining about a district decision and trying to change it. She wants to understand. She wants to learn why decisions were made and the purpose behind how this particular initiative unfolded. I appreciate her fire to reach a certain level of understanding. So much so that I take a step back and reflect.

Challenging administrative decisions might not be well-received by some, but this is the kind of challenge that I appreciate. It lets me know that as a leader, my implementation was not successful. While I may have thought that things were explained well or time was allotted to address teacher concerns, the reality was that it wasn't.

As leaders, it's easy to become defensive or push right back. Some might even shut down or consider retaliating against a teacher who challenges the boss, but if we have taken the time to build relation-ships with our teachers, then it doesn't become negative. If we are reflective in our leadership style, then we are pausing to consider what was said and how we can be accountable.

Jacie is right... I did need to vent, but it was more than that. I wasn't looking to blow smoke. I wanted to vent without judg-ment and personalization of the topic. I needed to have a real talk without my words being analyzed and with someone who knew me well enough to know I was coming from a good place... my heart! I needed to speak without fear that someone was going to relay my words incorrectly to another individual, as that has happened to me before. This was Jacie's initiative. This was something she valued tremendously and was trying to execute for the betterment of every child. I wasn't venting about Jacie, and she knew that... I was venting about the hurdles that were placed in front of every educator. I wanted to find a way to get over each of them to create a change of positive impact.

Part of it was that as much as I agreed with the new concept, I did not understand many of the things that were rubbing most of my colleagues and me the wrong way. Why was it being pushed out before we as educators were schooled on it? Why were we rushing to make a change that we were ill-informed to back up? Why were we not given time to do the job correctly so that it didn't take each of us 3-4 hours to complete? I had questions, and I needed answers. The honesty and humility that Jacie had in receiving my concerns and questions created an even stronger bond between us. She took the time to reflect on her own decision without the urge to defend her position. At no point did she address me in the way of, "I am your boss, and you need to comply" type of mentality. This was a true reflection of what leading looks like... or at least what I see as a leader. Her focus was on the learners, and she never wavered. She took my questions, my fears, my concerns, and she answered them with honesty and humility that was game-changing for me.

At this point, it was done. The new report cards were out there, and there was no turning back, but to be able to talk about the walk we were on together was valuable in the journey that was ahead of us. We realized yet again that the road we were traveling on would have its bumps and turns, but we were not in it alone. We had one-another to validate concerns and revamp what may not be working. This was yet another moment of trust that connected us and pushed us to forge ahead together for every child.

 JACKPOT!

In supportive relationships between teachers and admin, sometimes, you need to challenge the pit boss. Engaging in discussion and pushing back around important ideas is a critical part of moving your school forward.

DOUBLE DOWN

- As administrators, how can we set a tone in our buildings so that challenges are welcomed and create value for everyone involved?
- As teachers, how can we set a tone in our classroom so that challenges are welcomed and create value for everyone involved?

ANTE UP with Don Sturm

When I changed roles from a classroom teacher to technology integration specialist, I was a known commodity in my district. Decisions about student technology use have the potential to cause some discord between administration and myself. Most of the time the district administration and I have seen eye-to-eye on technology-related topics. When disagreements arose, I was lucky to have built up a level of trust where the administration had felt comfortable deferring to my "expertise." However, there is one area where I have not made any headway. In my district, students are not allowed on any social media platform while using their 1:1 iPad. I want to change that, but I have met resistance for the last five years about this topic. We discuss the importance of teaching digital citizenship, but I think it is hard, if not impossible, to teach those skills in a vacuum. I struggle with the fact that the lives of students is so closely tied to social media, but we play no part in it. Their school life is completely separate from their online life. This ongoing disagreement has allowed me to see the complexity of the relationship between school and home life that administration has to navigate on an ongoing basis. I respect the fact that the administration has a different perspective based on community input and expectations. I will continue to "fight" for the ability of our schools to help students navigate the online world, but I do this out of respect and not anger.

- Don Sturm, Technology Integration Specialist in Morton, Illinois
- Follow on Twitter @SturmDon

BET 22: HIT ME!

The Pit Boss Perspective

Our relationship as admin and teacher has had its moments
of truth over the last few years. We are at a point where
*we are honest with each other, even when our honesty is not going to
go over well with the other. It's tough when you have to give someone
feedback that they don't want to hear. As much as I want to provide
positive support whenever I can, there are times when you have to hit
them with the truth--even when they don't want to hear it.*

*It's back-to-school time, and the building principals have asked all
teachers to ramp up their communication with parents. In an effort
to be more responsive, the principals have selected a tool that teachers
will be required to use. For many teachers, this is a helpful tool, and it
allows them to provide ongoing feedback to students and parents. For*

others, this tool works in contradiction with the established positive classroom management systems.

While the mandate was well-received by most teachers, it was not welcomed by all. Here comes another Vox.

I listen. I imagine how I would have felt as a classroom teacher. Would I want to be told what tool to use? No. But there is another side to this. As an administrator, I need to back the decisions of the principals. Every elementary teacher is going to use this tool. Should I step in here or let it ride? I don't know if that's what she's looking for, but I feel like my intervention could solve the problem.

This is one of the times that having a strong relationship with a teacher makes things sticky.

As Jacie soon figured out, I was not looking for her to fix it as much as I was looking for her to see how this initiative was completely going against the one that she was valuing the most... breaking down the walls in learning. This was not personal. I had no idea who was pushing this initiative out; I simply needed understanding. I wanted to appreciate the value behind this decision so that I could embrace and execute it with ownership. I wasn't looking for the kind of *understanding* that comes with *"do it because you were told to,"* but the kind that would tell me how it was going to serve my students best. We had just been given permission to get on social media three years prior, and now we are being asked to jump into a silo of communication that would not only take steps back from connecting our parents and students to global learning but for us as educators too! From my perspective, and that of other colleagues, this simply did not jive with the path it appeared our district was taking.

I already had a plan in place to communicate with parents and one that worked well. I am all for change if it is for the better, but to change just for the sake of change makes absolutely no sense to me. My parents were finally following their child's work on Twitter and Facebook. They were seeing the abundance of educators nationwide commenting on what their child was learning and producing. It was incredible! It was liberating! It was a game-changer! And now it was about to come to a halt. **But Kristen, you can still tweet out your work with your students...** I was reassured.

Here is the thing, my push back on this initiative was for many reasons. In addition to feeling it was a step backward in breaking down the walls in learning and communicating, I need to keep balance in my life too. I was open to the concept, but not fully, as it did not offer a well-rounded opportunity as social media does. I know I was told I could still post ideas on other platforms, but this particular one was not linked to others; therefore, I would have to find time to do double, triple the work. I am a wife, a mother, a daughter, sister, friend, aunt, and teacher, a virtual co-op, and more. I am only given 24 hours to work with every day, and I am unable to connect with everyone I would like to within that day's time. Posting within meant minutes, I was not tweeting out work and connecting with a larger audience. I was no longer doing Tweet Challenges in class that my kids thrived on the year before... their very own authentic audience that connected them to others around the world! Done! Gone!

And for what? It Hit Me... I must be a professional and comply.

The upswing to the hit I just took was understanding. Jacie helped me to see it from a different perspective. She wasn't defensive about my questions, and she respected that I had something to add to the big picture. It wasn't a "just do it" and be a compliant conversation; it was an open forum to understanding where different voices were welcomed and appreciated. In turn, complying came with the support of more information, and it helped me to see it from another perspective. I walked away, ready to give it everything I had. My mindset had shifted, and I was ready to make it work for everyone involved. It hit me; open conversations of vulnerability mixed with a reservation on a judgment can be one of the most innovative approaches to education.

 **JACKPOT!**

Relationships are critical, especially at times of conflict or simple differences in viewpoints. It *"hit us"* that being able to talk through this conflict without personalizing viewpoints was critical for understanding, respect, and ultimately the success of any initiative. In the end, agreeing to disagree, is maybe the most respectful way of handling both sides. Walking away with an appreciation for the other's viewpoint is a *"hit me"* moment that will pay forward!

DOUBLE DOWN

- What tips do you have for successfully navigating these types of challenging conversations?
- How do you open yourself up to pushback that can propel you forward?
- When was the last time you faced a tough conversation face to face in place of an email or a phone call? Make your conversation a priority and place it on the calendar for a heart to heart talk!

ANTE UP with Sue Moyer

Relationship-building is the cornerstone of success. That success comes from hard and consistent work. Many of the relationship-building practices that I use begin with just listening and being present. That seems like such an easy concept, and it is, but the actual application takes effort and it is ongoing.

I became a superintendent of a school district which has been struggling for years, and I was named to the position during the last quarter of the year. My first job after being hired: listen. Listen to every stakeholder who would speak to gain a true appreciation of what they have done and what they saw as the future. It was during these listening sessions with the different stakeholders that relationships began to be built. These relationships are not just with the teachers and staff. They are with parents, community members, school board members.

One of the biggest things that I have learned from building relationships is that people want to hear a vision. These stakeholders want to know if my vision for the school district matches theirs. I need to be proud of the current accomplishments of our staff and students and share how those accomplishments are a part of my vision for the future of the district. I need to share that vision with confidence, understanding that there may be setbacks, but that we will continue to move forward.

- Sue Moyer, Superintendent in Duquesne, Pennsylvania
- Follow on Twitter @DukesSupINT

BET 23: JOIN THE PLAYER'S CLUB

The Pit Boss Perspective

*W*hen you join the Player's Club at a casino, the more bets you make, the more rewards you can earn. In education, taking risks isn't always rewarded, but maybe it should be. When educators are willing to step up and out of their comfort zones, not only are they stretching and growing, but by default, so are their students. As an administrator, I love watching this happen.

I work with a group of educators who represent five different school districts across our county. Teachers are invited into the consortium as a cohort of learners--sort of like the Player's Club. They commit to shared professional development for a two-year period, and the consortium leadership team commits to supporting their instructional risk-taking in both professional and financial ways. We have been lucky to work with three cohorts of teachers through this organiza-

tion. Many of them have taken the opportunity to engage in this work and expand upon it, leveraging their professional learning beyond what was expected.

One group created a conference proposal and presented it at a state conference as a cross-district team. Think about that--teachers working across boundaries to make a difference in their own learning and the learning of their students. That is powerful stuff!

At the conference, the team had time to network with other educators and leaders. They socialized with other educators and leaders across the state--others who were already in the Player's Club. They saw the impact that professional growth could have on them, especially when they surrounded themselves with others who were also interested in improving their practice.

The Player's Club has an open-door policy. It is not created for the elite, but more so the willing. It is designed with a variety of options and purposes and never disappoints on the return. It isn't about one set of people or one set location. It is a mindset that is put into action. It is about being a part of something that is

beyond the classroom,

beyond isolated thoughts,

beyond an individual ability.

Just like the Player's Club in the Casino, it isn't your age, your experience, or your attire, that gets you "in"; it is your willingness to take the risk, the relentless pursuit of hitting the jackpot, or even the positive energy that you bring to others that lifts the entire room to a new level.

The Consortium Club

I have been blessed to be a part of the county consortium with Jacie. This experience was limited in duration, but limitless in impact. It was just what I needed at a time in my career that I felt complete disappointment in myself for being stagnant in my own learning and that of my students. It was the open door that I needed to gain a new perspective and ideas that were coming from a variety of educators that carried a vast array of roles within their district. I was engulfed in positivity. I was leaving each meeting with the excitement of a better tomorrow. I couldn't wait to get back into my classroom to try a new spin on a lesson that was just shared out with me. Where had these people been? Why hadn't we connected before? I could have kept questioning the idea of the past and the disheartening disconnect I had had for so many years, or I could embrace the moment, re-energize myself, and create a new wave in education that my students and I needed so desperately. Embrace and empower is exactly what I did, **and with zest.**

The Book Club

I carried the energy from one club to the next. I set up book studies to share with others who needed this same rich experience. I decided to join book studies beyond my own district, state, and even country. This was absolutely mind-blowing, and I found myself spending more and more time at the club... the place that sparked excitement and had an ongoing return on my investment that would pay forward to every student and colleague alike. This club went from a book study to a family of unconditional support. We went from reading one book together to dozens. The spark was lit with Rich Czyz's book, The Four O'clock Faculty: A Rogue Guide to Revolutionary Professional Development, but it blew up into a bonfire that turned into #4OCFpln.

If you are looking to join a book study, contact #2menandabook co-creators Matthew Larson on Twitter @mlarson_nj and Ricardo Garcia @rokstar19 for more information.

The Voxer Club

There are times when I run out of minutes in a day and wonder how I will be able to get back in the club and feel the buzz that other enthusiastic educators feel. This is when I jump into Voxer. An app that has connected me globally with powerful, priceless minds. This club is open 24 hours a day and always aligns with someone's time zone at any point in the day. The beauty is that I can come and go based on my schedule and my need. It has given me the chance to sit down and mingle with teachers of all levels, administrators, tech integrators, curriculum instructors, pre-service teachers, professors, people in business, and so many more. It is a way to feel as if the person is sitting right next to you, as you are listening to their voice and can feel their excitement and emotion with every word. Connect one-on-one or find a group that meets your needs. A few to pick from would be:

4OCFpln

EduMatch

Restorative Justice League

The Conference Club

The impact of the right conference has always been a game-changer, but the effect of the players has created forever-changing possibilities. The time that you gain to collaborate with passionate educators who are striving towards similar goals is priceless. You are no longer grouped by grade level or title. You are in a club built on influential players that often build your professional learning network. Your common interests and energy create a bond, and in turn, you find yourself re-entering the upcoming school days with the power of players destined to impact every child and the trajectory of education as a whole.

"The Player's Club" offers as much as you are willing to take. Building relationships with the players within the club will always be a risk, but one worth taking. Allow your mind to be open to different viewpoints, push back with a new perspective, and encourage yourself to listen and engage as the conversations unfold.

 **JACKPOT!**

Being a part of a group may be just what you need to move your school or district forward. Build relationships with those who will support you in your mission and invite them into the Player's Club, whichever type of club works for you.

DOUBLE DOWN

- How might you build collective capacity with those around you and invest in improving your practice?
- What kind of "club" might you create that can encourage others and provide motivation for many?

ANTE UP with Vanessa Schreiber

As a teacher, I always tell my students "ask three before me." Children are to ask three friends to help them if they are stuck with independent work before coming up to me. I regimented this practice to build independence and interpersonal skills between my students. However, at the beginning of my teaching career, I did not heed my own advice. I believed I had to have it all figured out, after all – that's what teachers do. They have the answers and they deliver the knowledge, right? WRONG!

Into my second year, I started to become a member of the "player's club." I joined collaborative communities and experiences that my district offered. When I got there, I was nervous, young, and intimidated. During my first "player's club", I took away a lot of information. Most importantly, I learned that as teachers, we are stronger when we are together.

Teaching can be a very lonely practice. You are in a classroom all day with little people or adolescents that consistently depend on you. The only sounding board you have for your questions and decisions is yourself. When I entered the club, I found that there were professionals with the same questions as me. There were others with questions that piqued my curiosity. Some even pumped me up with their enthusiasm so much, that I wanted to be them! I felt like a brand new human!

While we all do our best to support each other in our districts, becoming a player has let me talk to other professionals across our county. It has provided me with an insight into education that I would not have gotten inside the walls of my classroom. I got to collaborate with people who taught different grade levels and content areas , and guess what?! They had some amazing insight and ideas! I didn't have to have all the answers like I originally thought! I just needed to know where to ask.

As I walked out, an official player of the club, I smiled, realizing I had bet it all for my students and hit the jackpot.

• Vanessa Schreiber, Autistic Support Teacher, Hopewell, Pennsylvania

- Follow her on Twitter @vanessaschreib4

ANTE UP with Melissa Rathmann

I joined Twitter in 2015 when I began hearing about the value of Professional Learning Networks. Twitter provided me with a network of people and resources to support ongoing learning while removing geographical barriers. After several years of following educators from across the world and building my #PLN, I realized that there was so much tweeting about what's wrong in education and not enough about what is right.

It was then that I decided there was a need for a chat that focused on celebrating our calling and each other. So, in the summer of 2018, #CelebratED was born! I reached out to members of my #PLN with the idea and began recruiting them to be a part of what I refer to as "The Mod Squad." Although many of the guest moderators have changed, the vision has not. We are a #PLN that supports, lifts, and celebrates one another. We focus on all of the amazing things educators across the world are doing to empower students and make our schools a better place. Please join us for #CelebratED each Wednesday night at 8:30 pm CST.

- Melissa Rathmann, Administrator, Curriculum and Instruction Specialist in Hutto, Texas
- Follow on Twitter @MelissaRathmann

BET 24: TIP THE DEALER

The Pit Boss Perspective

*W*hen things are going well at the poker table, we may throw some chips to the dealer. We acknowledge their encouragement in the game and give them a tip for their service. While the dealer doesn't have any control over who wins or loses, they play a critical part in the experience of the game.*

In education, we need to remember to throw some tips to those who make our game more enjoyable. The players who support us, the team that works hard, or the risk-takers who are out there pushing the limits every day. We need to give credit where it is due.

One thing that we started to do in our district was inspired by Mr. Rogers. Everyone's friend and neighbor, Fred Rogers was from Pittsburgh. His history was recently captured in an exhibit at the Heinz History Center. After an administrator field trip (yes, we go on field trips and try to have fun, too!), we were inspired by Mr. Roger's story. We began to think about all of the modern-day Fred Rogers who walk through schools each day, the teachers, paraprofessionals, bus drivers, custodians, and food service staff who greet us every day with a friendly smile and a kind word.

We celebrated these people at our opening day events and again for our end of the year events, shining a light on the individuals who do so much to lift others up, never looking for recognition. Just as you celebrate a win at the poker table by tipping the dealer a few chips at the end of a great run, we need to remember to do the same in our schools. "Tip" those around you who make your school a better place. Tip those who give selflessly to others, never looking for anything in return. Tip those who least expect it. Tip those who make your school a better place, just for being in it. Thank them. Celebrate them. Encourage them.

Encouragement can come in many forms:

a warm smile,

a needed hug,

a written note,

an uplifting email,

a listening ear, or

simply hearing the words, "good job."

Having someone in your corner as you navigate daily tasks or uncharted territory is what makes the world go around. None of us can escape a rough morning or a shift in tolerance levels that leaves us on edge with something that may not typically do so. When this happens, a friendly smile or a reminder of the positive impact you are creating can redirect your entire day. You can even surprise yourself as you may have felt that your day was gone before you even had a chance to start, but then you enter your classroom to find a note of encouragement to offset it all. Or maybe it is the colleague that sticks their head in the door "just" to check on you.

Rewards and acknowledgment are not at the forefront for most, but when it happens, you can't help but have your heart swell with a sense of love and pride. When you go from being focused on the betterment of your students to having someone focus on you, it leaves you with a sense of accomplishment that fuels your next move. The move that takes learning in a new direction because you know you can do it. The move that is taken with confidence because you know you are believed in. The small token handed to you has now stacked up, and you find yourself set to cash in over and over again.

There is no doubt that the same goes for students. The debate goes back and forth between intrinsic and extrinsic motivators. I could quote the experts or share my opinion, but instead, I push you to up the ante and try it yourself. See what sticks. See what your students need. Is it a...

pat on the back,

hug or high-five,

compliment for a job well-done,

moment of being noticed for the kindness they just shared,

note of encouragement,

celebration for their light bulb moment just created in their learning, or

a listening ear?

Go and create an impact... someone needs you!

 JACKPOT!

Tipping the dealer means recognizing others in the way that works for them. In addition, it means giving credit where it is due. This can happen at the district, school, or classroom levels. Toss an extra chip to those at the table who deserve some recognition--it will go a long way!

DOUBLE DOWN

Reflect on someone in your EDU circle who needs recognition.

- How will you acknowledge their efforts?
- In what way can you ensure that they know the impact they are making?

ANTE UP with Jeff Kubiak

Education is an interesting world. At times, it seems we are "all in" and together for #AllKids, no matter what. Then, on the other days, we actually compete against each other! Really? Aren't YOUR students, my students? I thought we were on the same team, pushing for each child to get what they need to fulfill any dream they wanted to reach for? Maybe more than one person wrote a book with similar content, genre, or information. Perhaps, there were some mutually beneficial blogs that may have shared some possible collaborative ideas What if two educators, in different continents, were presenting a keynote or PD and they actually mentioned similar research or data? HOLY COW!

Folks, we must compete TOGETHER. Our kids need this. We need this. Our country needs this! I understand that we need to earn a living and that sometimes we bid for the same work. But, with the work we need to do, as a whole, to get our students ahead of the curve and prepared for the future of the unknown, it must be a completely collaborative and team effort. I'll cheer for you, always. Yes, we need to post a pic of other's books. We must comment on our neighbor's blogs (after we actually read it!). Even though our time is sacred, and days speed past us, it is imperative that credit is given where it is due. Think about what would happen if this went away. Me for me. You for you. Them for them. Lose/Lose in my book.

Let's drop the egos. Focus on the child. Celebrate the blackjack winner, and band together. Now. Together. For all kids. One world. United.

- Jeff Kubiak, Educator, Author of *One Drop of Kindness*, Advocate for All Students
- Follow on Twitter @jeffreykubiak

ANTE UP with Sean Gaillard

In another life prior to becoming an educator, I played guitar in various bands. Most of these bands were pick-up and many of our gigs centered around the college campus coffee circuit. Most of these were not very good, but when we would hit a particularly good note or end a song on time, I would share the compliment in the following phrase, "You are making it happen!" This moment would serve as a catalyst for peaceful collaboration amidst the mania of the band struggling to get through a gig. I learned quickly that positivity could serve as a balm of encouragement for our struggles as a band. Encouragement would serve a sure bet for any band that I was lucky to have an affiliation.

I carried this lesson into my journey as a school leader. It is vital to recognize that we are a small part of the sum for a beautiful tapestry that envelopes a school's culture. There are many bandmates who add beautiful music in service and support of the kids we serve. Everyone in the schoolhouse must feel like they are a part of the band. There are many keys to play in order to recognize the valuable contributions our collaborators add.

There are a couple of ways that I strive to make this happen. I begin every faculty meeting I facilitate with what I call "Praise and Thanks." Simply put, this is the shoutout portion of the faculty meeting. I shine that spotlight on my colleagues who are making it happen for our kids. A simple word of praise and gratitude can go a long way to solidifying the positive culture we want each other and our kids to thrive. Another way that I celebrate the contributions of the teachers I serve is to make a Positive Principal Phone Call Home. I know that there are many principals who do this for kids and I count myself in those ranks. I think it is important to extend that warmth to our colleagues for a job well done. Nothing beats the expression on a teacher's face when you come in interrupting class to celebrate a gift they shared with our schoolhouse.

When you bet on the positive, everyone wins in the schoolhouse.

• Sean Gaillard, Principal of Moore Magnet Elementary School in Winston-Salem, North Carolina, Author of *The Pepper Effect*
• Follow on Twitter @smgaillard

BET 25: BEWARE OF THE LOAN SHARK

*B*ecause my teacher friends are under scrutiny at all times, I expect a lot from them—probably more than I expect from others. I expect that they are going to go above and beyond in all that they do. There is no room for someone claiming favoritism. Prove that you can take this chance and turn your stack of chips into so much more. Just like a loan shark, I have shared with them an opportunity to do something great. Try a new tool. Go to a conference. Take some risks. I am confident that they will do amazing things, but there is a small part of me thinking, "I gave you the OK-- please don't screw it up."

You have this opportunity. A second chance. What will you do with it? I don't want to have to come back and collect like a loan shark. I want the investment that I make in you to multiply and grow. I want to see the impact that the initial investment creates within you, your classroom, your students, and our community.

This is part of the risk that administrators take when they connect personally with teachers. When we publicly say, "this teacher is doing great things," it has the potential to put a target on those individuals and forces them to up their game. I am confident that they will, so I continue to invest in remarkable teachers.

Oh, "the second chance!" Such a gift that comes with the weight of the world. I mean, what is the worst thing that could happen, I fail miserably? Um, yep! That is a nightmare when you are balancing your innate risk-taking ability with respect and adoration you have for someone that believes in you!

And let's understand the implication of "second chance." It implies I needed one possibly due to a fault of my own, a moment that I did not live up to or even something else...

However, I didn't do any of those things. Actually, I was one of the ones who was keeping my students at the forefront and determined to give them every opportunity education could afford. The reality is, I was only able to give so much because there was very little trust being loaned out before Jacie's arrival in my district. What she felt was a second chance given to me was, in many ways, my first. Nonetheless, it was a loan of trust given to me, and I did not want to owe her anything in the end.

Truth be told, a chance is all I needed, and one I will never take for granted. Jacie gave me a chance. Through that chance, another one was afforded. From that chance, a friendship was formed. By taking the chance given and making something happen, trust was gained. Whether it was a chance that ended in success or failure, Jacie trusted that I would have takeaways to better myself and my students.

When Jacie says, "Don't screw it up," to me, that means don't waste the moment. Don't walk away from the experience with the same knowledge, the same mindset, and the same ability. Find value in the chance and grow... for your students, your colleagues, our community, and you! In the end, growth pays off the loan and leaves you debt-free!

The question now is, who is **your** loan shark?

Is it your...

Superintendent?

Assistant superintendent?

School Board?

Parent-Teacher Organization?

Community?

Secretary?

Custodial Staff?

Your family?

Your STUDENTS?

 **JACKPOT!**

Invest in those around you. The time and care that you put into others matters and will create change for the better.

DOUBLE DOWN

- **What is one area that you may need a second chance?**
- **What will you do with that opportunity?**

ANTE UP with Ty Jodon

Change is something that needs to happen in education. We, teachers, want the best for our students, so we need to be willing to update our mindsets and adopt new styles of teaching for what is best for the kids we see today.

My administration team asked me if I wanted to take on becoming the STEM teacher for our elementary buildings. I was uplifted by this opportunity because I knew they were making an investment that I have been wanting to be a part of ever since I started implementing STEM projects within my math classes. No pressure at all, right?

I asked my administrators a million questions and what they had in mind for our future STEM program, but all I ever received back was that they wholeheartedly believed in my judgment and creativity for what was best for our students. I didn't want to fail at this. Was I nervous about it? You better believe I was, but this is every teacher's dream, to be handed the reins for directing which way you wanted the journey to go.

I read blogs, joined consortium groups, reached out to other STEM teachers, took classes, and did everything under the sun to give my students the best STEM classes that I could provide and to show my dedication. Educators need to communicate with outside resources and have conversations about the good and bad things going on within their classrooms. I am the type of person who doesn't hesitate to walk into my administrator's office when I feel the need to talk about what I have in mind without actually scheduling a time to sit and talk. Keeping an open line of communication with my administration is what benefited me the most in this initial year of developing the STEM program because there was constant feedback from both sides. There were some growing pains, but my administration never once needed to come and collect on their investment. Keeping a positive growth mindset has also really helped me come out on top of this whole gamble.

I built a program that I felt fit our students and took it beyond the four walls of my classroom and invested in community programs. My passion for education has gotten me to where I am now because of the risks that I've been willing to take through the support of my administration.

- Tyler Jodon, STEAM Teacher in Beaver Falls, Pennsylvania

ANTE UP with Tonya O'Brien

Great leaders ignite sparks in others. These tiny sparks are visions that are apparent to some but are often tough to see or believe in oneself. There have been a handful of times in my life that a "loan shark" has invested in me and each time I have risen to the occasion.

One of the most significant investments was my call from administration to step out of my classroom and join an extended group of professional educators that stretched beyond my school or my district. In this mix, teachers and administrators worked side-by-side to build relationships and improve learning experiences. This journey took me out of my comfort zone and placed me directly into the fire.

Enthusiastically uncomfortable. Those are the best words to describe how participating in this project felt. Surrounded by many strangers and a few familiar faces, professional interactions pushed us to be better, to think harder, and to take risks. In this mix of colleagues, I uncovered my own "spark" that had been hidden away, the spark that my loan shark could see. I formed valuable relationships with fellow academic professionals built on mutual respect. The lines of "us" and "them" were blurred and what was apparent was the people and their passion for teaching, learning, leading, and supporting. This "bet" on me paid off tenfold and has positively impacted who I am as a teacher, a leader, and as an individual.

- Tonya O'Brien, Elementary Teacher in Hopewell Area School District, Pennsylvania

BET 26: DON'T GO BANKRUPT

The Pit Boss Perspective

*W*hen gamblers are on a roll, their pile of chips starts to grow. They keep rolling the dice. The excitement builds. Then all of a sudden, the losing streak begins. The fear of losing it all is looming. Any player can easily go bankrupt if they aren't staying on top of their game.

In education, we risk the chance of going bankrupt as well. If we don't take time to practice self-care, we will lose it all, including our sanity. As administrators, we have busy schedules, days full of meetings, and late nights with district activities and more meetings. In a world where we are always connected and accessible 24 hours a day, our days are different than the work of classroom teachers, but we come home exhausted just the same.

It is easy to go bankrupt and deplete ourselves of all energy and enthusiasm if we don't find ways to rejuvenate ourselves and take care of our mind, body, and spirit. For administrators, this might mean a mid-day walk through a building or around the school grounds. Stepping out to get some fresh air or getting out from the four walls of the office can provide a much-needed break.

When it's a scheduled board meeting night, I know I am going to work at least a 16-hour day, I have to take some time for myself or I know I will be bankrupt by the 7 pm meeting start time. I know I need to create some balance between work and life. How can we find ways to balance ourselves and create opportunities to get out of the red and into the black? How can we not only take care of ourselves but also ensure that our teachers don't go bankrupt?

"By investing in ourselves, we double the return for our students."

#ALLinEDU

I feel that when you are passionate about something, that in some way or another, you will create bankruptcy for yourself. When your time and attention are leading to growth and innovation, you can't help but lean in and take it for a ride. It is like stepping onto the Vegas ride, The High-Roller, and embracing every second that takes you to the top, but inevitably, you will come back down. Was it worth it? Often, we say YES without hesitation. But there are times we go too far, and we find ourselves wondering just how we will rebuild and pull it all together.

We must never forget who we are, what we are made of, and what we need to be at our personal best. Do we need to take time out and walk away from the intensity built around our role and impact? We are working with children, and that can never be taken for granted. Each child comes with a story. That story can make, break, or mask their ability. Through love, attention, and painstaking care, educators search for what is best for every child. It is through this relentless love that we find ourselves burning the candle at both ends. We do not shut off our love at the sound of the bell. They are our family, and, in many ways, they go home with us to make our once known family of four into a family of 25-30+ at any given point.

When we "take" our students home with us, we find that this responsibility manifests into struggles within our other roles. Being a mom, wife, sister, friend, and community member pushes me off balance, so when I need to recharge myself, I can never seem to get it just right. When I jump in and take the time to rejuvenate, I carry around the guilt that keeps me from being the best I can be in other facets of my life, and the cycle of imbalance continues. When I am giving everything that I have to all my roles, I slowly, but inevitably begin to exhaust myself. This is when I must have grace on myself. Once I do that, I can stop, reset, and restore. That may be time away from nightly work, which means the countless stacks of papers will have to wait for the next day. That may mean a break from social media and my PLN. (I thrive on their support and the support they give me, but there are times that I must remember that there are only so many hours in a day, and I must take time out of that allotment for myself to stop, reset, and restore.) That may mean not making a full spread dinner and simply order out. It may mean leaving the piles of laundry for the next day or even the next.

With this in mind, I must plan my summers to the best of my ability. Teachers often get so irritated when they feel judged for not giving up their summers for additional professional development. They already go days without breaks and often attend PD that they don't find value in, so this is definitely a hot topic in need of attention and understanding on all sides. Taking a walk in one's shoes is imperative. We simply don't know what each other's world looks like outside of the classroom. Most often, many are setting their own personal needs, family obligations, and overall mental well-being aside for that of their students. Many educators are focused on littles who

have broken homes

death in their families

illness for them personally and/or with family members

physical pain

emotional pain

learning hurdles and more!

Grace for ourselves

Grace for others

Self-help and worth.

Don't go bankrupt!

JACKPOT!

Take proactive steps so that you don't go bankrupt. Seek out ways to fill yourself up as well as those around you.

DOUBLE DOWN

- What do you do to practice self-care and ensure that you don't lose all your chips?
- How do you relate to those who have gone bankrupt?
- If you have gone bankrupt in the past, how did you reinvest to bring about change for yourself and others?

ANTE UP with Brittany Story-Stelzner

When I first started my profession, all I thought about was teaching. I stayed at school long after the bell and came home to an empty apartment, where I dreamed up lessons I couldn't wait to teach. I scoffed at the idea of burnout. That was for teachers who didn't really love their jobs. That was for whiners.

But then, I suffered a few tough years in my personal life. I carried the secret burden of infertility and miscarriage that so many women face. For the first time, I struggled to come up with ideas for class. I stared blankly at the computer and searched the internet listlessly for lesson plans. Teaching had been the music in my life, and now I was suddenly deaf to it.

The only thing that saved my love of teaching was taking a step back from it. I reduced my work hours. I took long walks with my husband. I let go of trying to be the best. I started meditating. After a while, I found myself daydreaming about lessons again. I laughed in class. I remembered how much I loved being with my students.

I continued meditating, long after that rough patch. This year, I wondered if giving my students a space to calm down could also help them. I instituted quiet reading time every day, with no exceptions. I put on calming music, turned off the lights and enforced quiet. At first, this caused a minor rebellion. But then, a surprising thing happened. My students started to read. Often, when the ten minutes came to an end, they begged for more time. One mother pulled me aside. "My kid is reading at home," she told me, incredulous, "For fun."

One reluctant reader plowed through a series about cats. "What have you done to her?" a teacher asked me at lunch, "I can't get a book out of her hands." I knew the experiment had been a success on the last wild day of school. I came into a room with the lights already off, spa music playing, and relaxed kids sprawled around the room, noses tucked into books. The room radiated calm. I smiled.

• Brittany Story-Stelzner, Middle School Teacher in Hopewell Area School District, Pennsylvania

ANTE UP with Elizabeth Merce

Giving your all is draining. It is impossible to give 100% of yourself without taking the time to take care of yourself. Self-care has become a buzz word in recent years and is now used any time someone wants to indulge. So what is self-care and how can we use it to make sure we stay healthy, focused, and motivated?

One could define self-care as the current you taking care of the future you. That means that self-care isn't always going to be about feeling good at the moment. In fact, some of the best kinds of self-care I've ever done have been things that were painful at the moment!

The first areas I always come to for self-care are physical and mental health. I lost a significant amount of weight after I got married 14 years ago and have been able to maintain it. This was not glamorous. It was not pleasant. It did, however, help me have more stamina and better focus. Making my physical health a priority also helped with my mental health. Treating your body well helps alleviate stress and gives you a positive outlet when you begin to feel overwhelmed. I still have to tell current Elizabeth to put down the Reese's. I'm not always successful, but future Elizabeth is always thankful when current Elizabeth listens.

Another domain that I focused on that wasn't glamorous but changed my life was financial. My husband and I chose our careers for the impact they would have on the community, not for the financial reward. That meant that we left college with low salaries and high loan balances. We put a huge focus on financial discipline and paid off $151,000 in record time. Our current selves are not always happy with the extra work or cutbacks needed, but our future selves are grateful.

You see our future selves ended up having a beautiful little girl who had medical issues. Eliminating financial stress in our lives helped us focus just on her healing. Did we plan on having a little one who needed extra care? No. Did discipline and hard work set us up for success? Yes!

Each day you have the choice to work through hard things so that the future you is healthier and more prepared. Make self-care about caring for yourself, in all areas. Self-care is only selfish when you focus on the current you and not the future you.

• Elizabeth Merce, Kindergarten Teacher/Adjunct Professor
• Follow on Twitter @EMercedLearning

BET 27: ALL IN

*W*e have all chosen to pursue our passions in the field of education. Although our pathways to get here may be varied and our roles may be different, we decided that this was a gamble that we wanted to take. The one worth taking. . . on our children! We grabbed our chips and chose a seat at the casino table. Our opportunity to make a difference is now.

The moment is there, right in front of you. You can feel your heart beating just a bit faster, and your hands start to sweat. The back of your neck feels clammy, and you reach back to wipe it as if that is all you need.

You are there.

You are feeling the moment.

The one that you know could have endless possibilities. The one that may be too radical for most. The one that you are afraid of for it may go south quicker than you can blink an eye.

Do you fold?

Do you walk away wondering what if?

Or are you ALL IN?

The stacks of chips are high. You had been working your way to this point for so long. It was becoming easier to just hold on to them. Your possessions, your winnings, your comfort zone, your world as you know it.

You push the chips to the middle. You don't even know what is making you do it. You are so scared that your hands are shaking, but you see yourself acting quickly before the chance gets away from you. Done.

By making this bet, you have taken a risk that can pay off in big ways. You push the doubts out of your mind and now stand at the table, confident in your decision. You have built positive relationships and surround yourself with players that are cheering you on. You got this!

You stand back.

You hold your breath.

You are there... ALL IN!

These moments are there for each of us every day. We must look for them. We must embrace them. We must act. We must go ALL IN for every child!

Be the one. Have the guts to do it. Fight the fear of not knowing if you will be successful or not. Just taking the opportunity gives you 100% more chance than the person who doesn't.

Step up. Push those chips in. Let the world take notice.

You are brave.

You are the risk-taker.

You exude confidence

YOU are **All In**!

"Relationships in education are critical. They require trust and at times a bit of a gamble, but most of all, a mindset that is "ALL IN!"

#ALLinEDU

KEEPING IT IN PERSPECTIVE

What role have you taken on?
Have you created an opportunity as the Pit Boss in your
learning space?
Are you willing to be a player, regardless of your role in
education?

*A*s with anything in life, views change with each perspective. As this journey unfolded between Jacie and Kristen, they too found their roles shifting and redefining. As Jacie initially took the lead as the "Pit Boss" and Kristen slid into the role of "player," they gained a working relationship that created opportunity, which in turn opened their minds to all possible roles of impact. Kristen found herself in the Pit Boss role when working with her students, fellow colleagues, the community, and even her administration. Not one of "boss," but one of a leader. Jacie found herself open to just the same, continuing to grow and learn as a player of the game. How is that possible, you may ask? As life-long learners, we come from one perspective, and as leaders, yet another. When we are "All In" with our students, these roles are not defined by age, degree, or title; they are roles of impact with the face of a risk-taker. Which side are you willing to take a risk to learn and lead from?

Pit Boss Perspective

Student
Community Member
Teacher
Administrator
Board Member

Player Perspective

Student
Community Member
Teacher
Administrator
Board Member

REFERENCES

Couros, G. (2015). *The innovator's mindset: Empower learning, unleash talent, and lead a culture of creativity.* San Diego, CA: Dave Burgess Consulting, Inc.

Goodreads.com/quotes/421800-gratitude-can-transform-common-days-into-thanksgivings-turn-routine-jobs

Merriam-webster.com. (2019). *Definition of EXCEPTIONALITY.* [online] Available at: https://www.merriam-webster.com/dictionary/exceptionality [Accessed 15 Jul. 2019].

Murray, T.C. (2018, December 29) How do you model risk-taking? [web log post] Retrieved June 2, 2019, from http://premierespeakers.com/thomas_murray/blog/2018/12/29/how_do_you_model_risk-taking

PBLWorks. (2019). *WHAT*. [online] Available at https://www.pblworks.org/what-is-pbl [Accessed 16 Jul. 2019].

Sheninger, E. (2014). *Digital leadership: Changing paradigms for changing times.* Thousand Oaks, CA: Corwin Press.

OTHER EDUMATCH TITLES

Unlock Creativity by Jacie Maslyk
Every classroom is filled with creative potential. Unlock Creativity
will help you discover opportunities that will make every student see
themselves as a creative thinker.

EduMatch Snapshot in Education (2016)
In this collaborative project, twenty educators located throughout the United States share educational strategies that have worked well for them, both with students and in their professional practice.

The #EduMatch Teacher's Recipe Guide
Editors: Tammy Neil & Sarah Thomas
Dive in as fourteen international educators share their recipes for success, both literally and metaphorically!

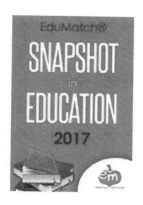

EduMatch Snapshot in Education (2017)
We're back! EduMatch proudly presents Snapshot in Education (2017). In this two-volume collection, 32 educators and one student share their tips for the classroom and professional practice.

Journey to The "Y" in You by Dene Gainey
This book started as a series of separate writing pieces that were eventually woven together to form a fabric called The Y in You. The question is, "What's the 'why' in you?"

The Teacher's Journey by Brian Costello
Follow the Teacher's Journey with Brian as he weaves together the stories of seven incredible educators. Each step encourages educators at any level to reflect, grow, and connect.

The Fire Within
Compiled and edited by Mandy Froehlich
Adversity itself is not what defines us. It is how we react to that adversity and the choices we make that creates who we are and how we will persevere.

EduMagic by Sam Fecich

This book challenges the thought that "teaching" begins only after certification and college graduation. Instead, it describes how students in teacher preparation programs have value to offer their future colleagues, even as they are learning to be teachers!

Makers in Schools
Editors: Susan Brown & Barbara Liedahl
The maker mindset sets the stage for the Fourth Industrial Revolution, empowering educators to guide their students.

Divergent EDU by Mandy Froehlich
The concept of being innovative can be made to sound so simple. But what if the development of the innovative thinking isn't the only roadblock?

EduMatch Snapshot in Education (2018)
EduMatch® is back for our third annual Snapshot in Education. Dive in as 21 educators share a snapshot of what they learned, what they did, and how they grew in 2018.

Daddy's Favorites by Elissa Joy
Illustrated by Dionne Victoria
Five-year-old Jill wants to be the center of everyone's world. But, her most favorite person in the world, without fail, is her Daddy. But Daddy has to be Daddy, and most times that means he has to be there when everyone needs him, especially when her brother Danny needs him.

Level Up Leadership by Brian Kulak
Gaming has captivated its players for generations and cemented itself as a fundamental part of our culture. In order to reach the end of the game, they all need to level up.

DigCit Kids edited by Marialice Curran & Curran Dee
*This book is a compilation of stories, starting with our own mother
and son story, and shares examples from both parents and educators
on how they embed digital citizenship at home and in the classroom.
(Also available in Spanish)*

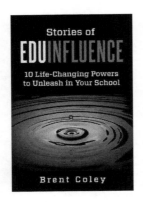

Stories of EduInfluence by Brent Coley
*In Stories of EduInfluence, veteran educator Brent Coley shares
stories from more than two decades in the classroom and front office.*

The Edupreneur by Dr. Will
The Edupreneur is a 2019 documentary film that takes you on a journey into the successes and challenges of some of the most recognized names in K-12 education consulting.

In Other Words by Rachelle Dene Poth
In Other Words is a book full of inspirational and thought-provoking quotes that have pushed the author's thinking and inspired her.

To Whom it May Concern
Editors: Sarah-Jane Thomas, PhD & Nicol R. Howard, PhD
In To Whom it May Concern..., you will read a collaboration between two Master's in Education classes at two universities on opposite coasts of the United States.

One Drop of Kindness by Jeff Kubiak
This children's book, along with each of you, will change our world as we know it. It only takes One Drop of Kindness to fill a heart with love.

DI in the Teaching Profession by Kristen Koppers
Differentiated Instruction in the Teaching Profession is an innovative way to use critical thinking skills to create strategies to help all students succeed.

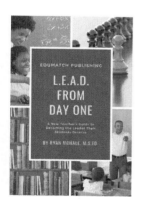

L.E.A.D. from Day One by Ryan McHale
L.E.A.D. from Day One is a go-to resource to help educators outline a future plan toward becoming a teacher leader.

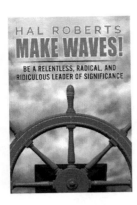

Make Waves! by Hal Roberts

In Make Waves! Hal discusses 15 attributes of a great leader. He shares his varied experience as a teacher, leader, a player in the N.F.L., and a plethora of research to take you on a journey to emerge as leader of significance.

21 Lessons of Tech Integration Coaching by Martine Brown

In 21 Lessons of Tech Integration Coaching, Martine Brown provides a practical guide about how to use your skills to support and transform schools.

EduMatch Publishing

Made in the USA
Lexington, KY
29 November 2019

57813146R00144